HOW HEART-CEN[...]
CHANGES THE WAY[...]

STEEL
BACKBONE
SOFT
HEART

CHERYL DESANTIS

WHAT PEOPLE ARE SAYING ABOUT

STEEL BACKBONE SOFT HEART

"As a leader, *Steel Backbone, Soft Heart* is a must read for empowering your role in today's business marketplace. Cheryl's heart-centered leadership will transform your life, career, and business while you discover the power of your empathic heart and the inner strength of your backbone."

– JAMES M. RINK
Speaker, Author, Television Producer + CEO,
Rink Entertainment, LLC

"Cheryl has consistently leaned into her personal and professional growth while courageously navigating complex systems and people over the years. She is committed to leading and living from her heart with wisdom, and many people and businesses have benefited from her leadership and approach to life. This book gives you practical tips and exercises to find your own heart-centered path."

– HELEN-JANE NELSON
Founder & CEO of Cecera Consulting Limited

"Cheryl DeSantis has written a must-read primer for anyone wanting to take their leadership to the next level. Steel Backbone, Soft Heart shares Cheryl's personal journey that has honed her transparent, real, and transformative style of leadership. Read this book and learn from one of the best on how to be the type of person that leads authentically, creates immense loyalty, and leaves a lasting legacy."

— CHRIS HAMILTON
President and CEO, Red Collar Pet Foods
& Founder, Borealis Partners, LLC

"Smart, insightful, strong, and compassionate, Cheryl has a way of kicking us in the ass while giving us an emotional hug at the same time. Steel Backbone, Soft Heart cuts through the BS of our mind's endless chatter and offers us a path toward true work/life harmony."

— JAMIE GEORGE
Author, Executive Coach
& CEO of Story Collector

"Today more than ever we need leaders who are willing to model what success can look like when you lead from the heart. It takes grit to be a leader, but it takes heart to elevate those around you. Steel Backbone, Soft Heart shows why these two powerful traits are critical for visionary leadership."

— JUDY WILKINS-SMITH
Author of Decoding Your Emotional Blueprint

Fedd Books
P.O. Box 341973
Austin, TX 78734

www.thefeddagency.com

Published in association with The Fedd Agency, Inc., a literary agency.

Design by Deryn Pieterse

ISBN: 978-1-949784-99-2

eISBN: 978-1-957616-00-1

Library of Congress Number: 2022901382

Printed in the United States of America

First Edition 22 23 24 25 /6 5 4 3 2

Some names have been changed to protect people's privacy.

To my daughters, Marlie, Jessie, and Ava,
may you always know you are enough just by
being who you are. Keep shining and changing the
world. One courageous step at a time.

To my mother, Jan,
you are the true hero in my story.

CONTENTS

ONLY HUMAN

Throughout 2020 and 2021, those of us in office jobs got a very different look at our coworkers. Whether it was kids running through the Zoom frame, the dog barking, or an elderly parent with a question, we saw more of each other's whole lives than we ever used to at the office.

And that's a good thing.

Of course, we knew before that we all have lives outside of work. But, as leaders, sometimes we have blinders on when we see employees only at the office. We know, logically, they must juggle outside pressures, but we don't feel that juggling or the toll it takes.

Employees also may feel the need to mask parts of who they are when they're at work. A Deloitte study found that 61 percent of employees downplay aspects of their personal lives at work.[1] This is primarily due to the environments that leaders create.

Leaders too often think it's the big things—like performance reviews and public recognition—that make the most impact on employees. But it's the small decisions every day that make people feel seen, heard, and respected. It's being intentional about recognizing and respecting a person's humanity and, from a work perspective, showing that you see how their humanity fuels their professional success.

We can't unsee what we saw on Zoom during quarantine. And what we saw is more of the whole person. When I think about the future of the business world, I believe the most significant determinant of a company's success will be its pursuit to recapture and appreciate its employees' humanity. According to the latest JOLTS report, a record number, 4.4 million, of Americans left their jobs in September 2021, accelerating a trend that has become known as the Great Resignation.[2] We can't keep pushing people to their limits to choose between work and life. Burnout doesn't have to be inevitable. This is where heart-centered leadership comes in.

Heart-centered leadership is about inspiring and motivating others from a complete understanding of everyone's humanity, purpose, and unique value. It's about leaders setting an example and inviting others into genuine connections and deeper relationships. Heart-centered leadership means having a steel backbone to get work done and a soft heart to ensure you are treating people with care and respect along the way.

Steel backbone, soft heart. Those are the keys to heart-centered leadership. Now, you may be thinking that a soft heart will fast-track you to getting taken advantage of—I hear you. And I've been there. At the end of the day, businesses need to earn a profit, serve customers and clients, and execute strategies for sales and growth. That's why having a steel backbone is an essential part of heart-centered leadership. Having a steel backbone doesn't take away from recognizing the humanity of the people around you; instead, it exists alongside that reality and helps you set goals, expectations, and deadlines that benefit the company and are agreeable and sustainable for the members of the team.

I used to think you had to be hard to be a leader—tough and driving. I over-indexed on the competitive side of my nature and didn't understand that this strategy could never help me create the followership I needed. I was building a winning team but not a loyal one. I wasn't showing them or me what I believed in. And I wasn't giving them the love and care that great leaders provide. This is the secret to leadership. Sure, you need to be capable, have vision, and set clear goals. But great leaders genuinely care about their people. They want to connect to their employees' hearts as well as their heads. Get to know their families, understand their origin and life stories, let them be vulnerable. It will drive a connection that no other parts of leadership can deliver.

My years in the corporate world have been serpentine. I have learned how to do things the easy way through good mentors and the hard way through terrible managers. I have worked hard, and I've seen the absolute necessity of empathy in the workplace. As I write this, I serve as the Chief People and Diversity Officer at SmileDirectClub, where I have made a point to lead with a strong backbone and soft heart. And I've found that heart-centered leadership doesn't compromise productivity or effectiveness; it encourages it. When we, as leaders, respect the humanity of our people, they, in turn, give back that humanity when we experience bumps in our businesses. This thinking is rooted in mutuality, which, in my view, is a fundamental aspect of leadership. The balance of giving and receiving makes situations a win-win.

Heart-centered leadership unlocks talent and enables higher performance. And, frankly, it's more necessary than ever for retaining a team. The world is changing around us. The old thinking that says leadership requires instilling fear, displaying toughness, or being bulletproof is over. The idea that empathy and compassion will lead you to the wrong end of turnover numbers has been disproven.

To practice heart-centered leadership in the workplace, we need to incorporate it into our personal lives. Your personal life and the relationships therein are an essential part of who you are, and to create a human-centric workplace, you must bring your whole self to the table. In this book, I want to empower you to live, love, and lead with a steel backbone and a soft heart. In each chapter, I will break down an essential principle of being a heart-centered leader. Then, through personal and professional examples from my own life, I will walk you through the necessity and application of each principle. At the end of each chapter, I will provide reflection points and questions to help you build your steel backbone and soft heart and become the most effective leader possible. I have changed the names of some in this book to protect their privacy.

We are approaching a seismic shift in work, and outdated

leadership is the first thing we must examine. When leaders encourage people to be unapologetically themselves, when we celebrate people's humanity in the workplace, we will experience more success, progress, and growth individually and as teams. This isn't a question of soft skills versus hard skills; it's about utilizing both to be a great leader and build a great team. You must be strong and capable yet open and full of heart. Steel backbone, soft heart. That is the winning combination, and we need more of this in corporate America.

CHAPTER 1

CURIOSITY

Uncover Your Origin Story

I have always been drawn to the hero's journey. Not because I felt like one, but because I could relate to the traumatic event that sent the hero on a journey to become something more than they believed they were or deserved to be. I'm not a hero, far from it. I'm just a person who has been handed both gifts and trauma and figured out how to weave them together into something positive.

We all write our own stories, and for better or for worse, we are the hero in our own stories. The most powerful things we do in the story of our lives are make meaning out of the things that happen to us and attempt to make sense of the world around us. That prescribed meaning dictates how we view ourselves, our lives, our work, and others. The mindsets, limiting beliefs, fears, and behaviors we pick up from events in our lives set our course and fill out our stories.

This habit of meaning-making and storytelling starts when we are children and grows with us throughout our lives, in every aspect. It affects the way we view ourselves, the way we lead, and how we show love to others. If we never address the stories we tell ourselves about ourselves, our stories will never evolve.

The first principle of heart-centered leadership is curiosity. Curiosity helps us reflect on where things are now, how they got there, and how we could improve them. When we're curious, we demonstrate initiative and interest, communicating care and dedication. The best leaders I've ever interacted with are endlessly curious about (1) people and (2) how they can improve systems.

First, let's focus on curiosity about ourselves, our stories, and how they tie into our leadership styles and personalities. We can do this by looking at our origin story and connecting the dots between our experiences of critical developmental stages of our lives and how they have played a role in the way we live, lead, and love today.

Every hero has an origin story, and though they aren't all as dark as Batman's, they tell us a lot about our perspective and responses. Often, the things that happened to us when we were children harden us. We build up an armor around our insecurities and fears, and we make sure no one will ever be able to penetrate that armor—especially at work. Looking back at your origin story and identifying the meaningful moments that steered you toward positivity or negativity are essential to your personal development. By identifying these moments, you can start to take off the armor that has helped you feel strong all these years and begin to recognize your inner strength. Doing so will enable you to have a soft heart and connect with others without your fear getting in the way.

How can you get more in tune with your life story, love story, and leadership story? Get curious about your beliefs and how you built them. To be your own hero, you need to know your origin story and what you made that mean. You will need to look within to determine how your personal story relates to your leadership style. The more you understand yourself, the better you can lead others.

When we get curious about our self-made stories and the stories of the people on our teams and how those stories affect our personal and professional lives, we are more equipped to lead with a steel backbone and soft heart.

IDENTIFYING MEANINGFUL MOMENTS

Here's a quick exercise adapted from the work of Tracy Goss to identify your meaningful moments and what you did with them:

1. Think of three painful memories from your childhood and write down a key word related to each memory. They can be from any age, 0-18. You can use this guide to pick one from the age of 0-7, one from 8-14, and one from 15-18. Write them down and remember how they felt. You might find that you have more painful moments in one age group than the rest, and that's okay too. You know you are on the right track when you can feel some emotion from the memory.

2. Next to each, write how you made meaning out of the experience and any promises you made to yourself from the experience.

3. Evaluate how those promises you made have played out in your life. Have they been empowering (winning formula) or diminishing (limiting belief)?

Keep this handy as we go through this book, as these meaningful moments are usually at the heart of our life and leadership stories. I will share my memories with you as we go.

MY ORIGIN STORY

"If you mess up, they will get rid of you too."

Those words haunted me for most of my life—whispered to me from the innocence of a child, yet burned into me like a visceral brand. I lived my life in fear that one wrong move would leave me homeless, without a family, and on my own. The day I heard these words, I derived from them the meaning that I wasn't safe and promised myself not to get on anyone's bad side and be perfect in all I do.

My journey to wholeness and finding my true self was not easy. My armor of invulnerability shielded me from a life of true acceptance, love, and, in the workplace, decisive leadership. My story starts with abandonment and rejection with a strong turn into perfectionism and isolation. I was living an inauthentic life, and it very nearly took me down.

I was born in New Brighton, Pennsylvania. How charming is that? It seems perfectly prophetic for someone with a relentless need to find the bright side of anything. I was the baby of a young girl whose parents felt it was not acceptable to have a pregnant teenage daughter. My biological mother, Barbara, was eighteen when she had me. She was from a wealthy family in Philadelphia, and when her parents found out she was pregnant, they decided to send her off to Pittsburgh to be looked after by a doctor friend, Dr. Crozier. Barbara had to stay in a hotel by herself, and Dr. Crozier would come by and make sure she was okay.

A special lady named Jan Willson worked with Dr. Crozier. Jan and her husband, Gordon, had one son, Eric, and then Jan struggled to have another child. Finally, after several miscarriages, she and Gordon decided on the path of adoption. Lucky for me, she was Dr. Crozier's first choice when the decision was made to offer Barbara's baby for adoption.

On December 18, 1969, I entered this world, and three days later, I left the hospital with Jan and Gordon. After living for nine months in Barbara's womb, Jan and Gordon brought me to a small town called Conway, Pennsylvania, to meet my new family—aunts, uncles, and cousins were all lined up on the street waiting to meet the latest addition. All were ecstatic, except maybe my new brother, Eric. He was only three at the time. His first words upon meeting me were "stand her up and let's see if she can walk." High expectations early on!

I don't remember much of my dad, Gordon, growing up. He was deployed to Vietnam two times and then left for Korea, so I don't recall ever living with him. My parents divorced when I was five. It was another painful early memory in my life. I remember the day he left. We lived in a tiny townhouse, and I came to the front door where my dad was hugging my mom, and my mom was sobbing, saying, "Don't go."

Gordon started a new family with his wife, Carmen, and they had a son, Gordon. From 1980 on, Dad lived in London, Germany, Hawaii, and Oregon. We did not see him very much, except for a few summer trips. Gordon felt and still feels like a distant relative to me. He's a sweet man, and I love him like a child loves a parent, but after the divorce, he just could not connect with Eric and me. The guilt got him. He was a great father to my half-brother, Gordon, and a great husband to Carmen. Eric and I just accepted that we didn't fit into his life. We felt secondary. This experience further instilled a fear of abandonment in me.

I didn't know I was adopted until I was about four years old. Jan had hung a pink felt wall décor in my room. It was a poem that read, "Not flesh of my flesh, nor bone of my bone, but still miraculously my own. Always remember you didn't grow under my heart but in it." My mom sat me down on my fuchsia carpet and explained it, and for the first time in my short life, I saw my life flash before my eyes. I tried to tell myself it was okay because I looked like my parents and people wouldn't know. I can remember going to my mom's work and people telling her I looked like her, which was reassuring to my little mind. I didn't want to be different, and I thought that if people found out I was adopted, they would not like or accept me. It was terrifying, and I didn't feel safe sharing this secret with anyone.

These events, being adopted, my parents' divorce, and hearing I could be evicted from my life, started shaping my worldview and self-image from a young age. My mind was full of fear and an inner drive to be perfect. I started telling myself stories that limited how I saw myself and what I thought I was capable of. I didn't trust anyone would be there for me, so I became self-reliant. I felt that achievement was the path to love. I would live out these patterns for years.

How we make sense of critical defining moments when we are young plays a considerable role in shaping our worldview. When we don't analyze them and realize their role, there is a bigger chance that they will negatively impact our leadership. By identifying key memories and their respective meanings, we can begin the work of unlearning limiting beliefs.

LIMITING BELIEFS

We are all meaning-making machines. Events happen that we can't control. What we can control is our reaction to them. However, our meaning-making is often rooted in our wounds, and our reactions can come from a narrow, limiting mindset. The traumatic or painful events in our origin stories create our primary fears, leading to limiting beliefs that affect our daily lives.

We take events and put our lens on them to understand and classify the world around us. My origin story started with a primal wound, which is often present in children who grow up without their biological parents. The theory presented in Nancy Verrier's book *The Primal Wound: Understanding the Adopted Child* says a baby knows when they are not with the mother who created them. The smells, the sounds, the sense of connection are off. It is why adoptees are often anxious or avoidant attachers—because that initial attachment was severed so abruptly. Adoptees have a double bind because they don't have their mother or father. Because of these reasons, many adoptees take on an inherent fear of abandonment. Still, this fear can also take hold of children with distant parents or children whose parent disappears following divorce.[3]

So, a big part of my journey has been about overcoming the ever-present sense of abandonment and feeling of not being good enough, which, for me, was rooted in adoption. I swallowed the story that I had to be perfect so I could prove to all that I belonged and am, indeed, wanted. This promise to myself drove me to be an achiever and a people pleaser. I had to be compliant. But the downside was too terrifying: expulsion from another family. So in this fight-or-flight moment, I chose to fight. I decided to become the perfect child, always smiling, trying not to be a problem. Our fears and limiting beliefs result in behaviors, and those behaviors build our weaknesses and our strengths. Not everything is negative. Because of the meaning I'd made about being adopted and my parents' divorce, I gained some valuable skills that are part of my winning formula in life. I started learning how to read people, events, and tones of voice to determine how others felt. By being quiet and observant, I learned the basics of people skills. Even though my original intent was to figure out if I fit in, my curiosity led me to understand how to read people. I focused on doing well in school and sports because I learned that achievement got a positive reaction. I began to thrive in these areas because I thought achievement equaled love, and I knew the playbook on how to improve. The stories I told myself helped me be incredibly successful because they embedded in me a deep desire to be the best. However, the pain of it was something I buried for years. The pressure I put on myself to be perfect was always too heavy to bear.

Sometimes limiting beliefs help you cope and get through seasons, but like most things, they have their periods of usefulness and you should regularly examine them to see if they still serve you. Think about the events in your origin story that have led to your primary fears and limiting beliefs. Once you recognize the stories you are telling yourself, you can begin to see the ways your story doesn't serve you. That is when you need to identify the truths and changes that will help you see your story in a more honest and compassionate light.

The model below helps you shape your story. I've included my details. Take the time now to write in your own.

Events: Adoption; parents' divorce; hearing that if I messed up, my family would get rid of me.

Primary Fear: Abandonment.

Limiting Belief(s): I need to be compliant and perfect to be loved and found worthy. I can't afford to make mistakes, and I can't rely on others. I have to be self-sufficient.

Behaviors: Learning how to observe and read people; masking my true emotions; a drive to achieve; trying to be the best at every possible thing so I won't be abandoned again.

Strengths: An inner desire to strive for excellence in everything; ambition

Weaknesses: Prioritizing others' opinions above my own; not speaking my truth; blending in with the environment to fit in.

Truths and Changes: I do not need to be perfect, compliant, or successful to be loved and accepted; I just need to be myself. I want to shift my focus from striving for excellence and success out of fear of abandonment to celebrating my gifts and drive.

BUILDING YOUR ARMOR

Creating meaning around the events in our lives impacts our mindsets and behaviors. I know now that my specific journey was a gift of epic proportions—being abandoned by my birth parents, suffering that primal separation wound—and learning how to take that pain and make it something special has been my biggest revelation. Getting to that sentence took a lot of hard lessons and pain, but they are lessons that have made me stronger and more compassionate.

Growing up, I directed my perfectionism and endless drive toward sports, which was a great outlet. And as I grew up, I directed my desire for success and approval toward my professional life. Pursuing everything with excellence and passion meant I moved up quickly during my career.

When I graduated, I wanted to be in public relations. However, I started my career during a recession, which meant taking whatever job I could get. My first job consisted of answering phones, but I soon moved into a marketing position. After two years at my first job, I moved into PR.

In my first PR job, the environment was more than slightly akin to the office environment in *Mad Men*. We all had offices, each with drawers of alcohol, and there was a deep collegiality of creativity. However, it was a little too volatile for me, so I switched to a very corporate company called Seabury & Smith. I moved into a role in corporate communications. It was a slight shift from PR, but I was able to leverage my writing skills. Here, I had the opportunity to get a master's degree in communications.

From there, I worked at MCI, a disrupter of the phone industry, taking on what we cheekily called the Death Star—AT&T. It was fun to work there, and I learned the joy in taking on the big competitor. We embodied the young upstart challenger mentality, a feeling I would return to later. We all worked hard and played hard. Here I got into HR communications, which was my first foray into Human Resources. Later I took a role in TV advertising and eMarketing (ironically, less like *Mad Men*). You may be starting to see a trend of decision-making at work in my career. Basically, I would ask myself, "Why not?" when considering a job; I was curious. I figured that if it was new and different, I would learn something. I wasn't concerned with a vertical experience except in title. I didn't mind being in different areas; I just wanted to keep getting more senior and more money. I developed my true leadership skills while working at Mars, Inc. and now at SmileDirectClub.

My background has been quite a patchwork, spending time in public relations, marketing, corporate communications, TV advertising, and HR. Yet, through all those roles, what set me apart was being a fast learner, eager to excel, a good teammate, and able to connect with people by focusing on them.

I survived by putting on armor to protect myself. I didn't want to share myself for fear of being rejected. And with my need to be perfect, I buried the person I was for the person I thought I needed to be: successful, perfect, career-oriented, compliant. I worked hard, prioritized diligence and integrity, and dared to go after new opportunities. But these benefits didn't come without their cost. I became a chameleon to fit in with whatever environment I was in, and I lost myself along the way.

Often, we build armor to protect ourselves. But there comes a time when we need to set down the armor and find the strength and confidence we need internally. The only way we'll be able to lead successfully is with empathy and confidence. So how do we take off this armor? If you've done the exercises thus far, you're already on your way.

***

So, what do origin stories and armor have to do with leadership? Frankly, everything. When we get curious and start looking at what makes us tick and why, we can gain a lot of insight into our strengths and weaknesses as leaders. Our origin stories and the meaning we make from them become foundational to our interactions with others, our work ethic, and our personalities. Understanding that we all have childhood wounds that affect how we live, love, and lead brings a sense of humanity back to the workplace.

For you and your team to step into your strengths and superpowers, you will need to get curious, go back to the beginning, and look at your origin story and the meaning-making you've done in your life story. For some, this might bring up feelings of shame or traumatic memories. I would encourage you to process through your origin story with a professional therapist or life coach if that is the case. But no matter what it brings up, it will begin the journey toward wholeness and authentic, heart-centered leadership. Once we realize the meaning, mindsets, and behaviors that have had a potent impact on our lives, we can analyze the strengths and weaknesses of those events and come up with a game plan for healthier responses and mindsets.

To be an effective leader, you don't need to know every aspect of every team member's origin story. Being curious about their values and upbringing will help you tap into effective leadership gracefully. Simply acknowledging that everyone has an origin story and being curious about them will help open your eyes to others' humanity. We may be meaning-making machines, but underneath all of that is a soft heart that wants to find love, acceptance, and belonging.

HEART-CENTERED LEADERSHIP LESSON
CURIOSITY

Steel Backbone:
We all have unique parameters and experiences to outgrow a limiting belief. By reflecting on our lives through the lens of curiosity rather than judgment or shame, we can gain more insight into ourselves.

What are your limiting beliefs, and how can you create a daily practice of overcoming them?

Soft Heart:
We all have an inner child who can teach us about our origin story and the hurts and beliefs we carry from it. When we think of our inner child, it becomes easier to be compassionate and gracious with ourselves.

Can you imagine your inner child? What would you say to them? What would they say to you?

CHAPTER 2

COMPASSION

Focus on Others

When we get curious and map out all the aspects of our origin stories, we become more compassionate with ourselves. Being more compassionate toward ourselves helps us be more attune and compassionate with those around us. It is a virtuous cycle. Compassion is the second principle of heart-centered leadership. This one is semi-intuitive, but it's important to define what compassion means and how to practice it in the different contexts of our lives, including with ourselves.

The best description I've read about compassion and how it shows up in our lives comes from the book *The Places That Scare You* by Pema Chödrön, an American Tibetan Buddhist and ordained nun. Pema says:

> *In cultivating compassion we draw from the wholeness of our experience—our suffering, our empathy, as well as our cruelty and terror. It has to be this way. Compassion is not a relationship between the healer*

and the wounded. It's a relationship between equals
. . . Compassion becomes real when we recognize our
shared humanity.[4]

Being a leader with a steel backbone and soft heart is all about understanding and celebrating our shared humanity. A vital aspect of that is having compassion for others around us. We need to learn to see others, develop empathy, celebrate diversity, and build trust through listening to do this well.

LEARN TO SEE OTHERS

In the hero's journey, there is always a wise mentor who comes along and guides and inspires them. Mentors are invaluable in our lives. They challenge us to grow, guide us in our decisions, and offer wisdom we have yet to gain.

I've had many mentors throughout my life, but the first mentor I ever had in life was Ed Duffy.

When I was nine years old, my mom introduced us to the man who would eventually change the trajectory of my life and who remains the role model for how I want to lead: Edward Michael Francis Duffy, Jr.—a man bigger than life itself, yet as approachable as they come. Ed had a deep booming voice. His natural charisma pulled in everyone around him. He could immediately connect with someone and make them feel like they were the only person in the room. He loved to make people smile.

My mom shared the story of their first date and how he came over in a car that can only be described as big and Flintstonian. He asked her to drive, which she did. When she looked down after taking the wheel, she noticed that pieces of the floor were missing and she could see the road beneath her—quite a colorful start, yet one that showed he had no pretense. He was sweet and funny with a twinkle in his eye—the epitome of an Irish showman.

Needless to say, my first encounter with him was eventful. One day, when Ed came to pick up my mom for a date, Eric and I were in the middle of a sibling squabble. I did something to make Eric mad, and he started chasing me, as brothers do. I ran out the front door, took a quick left, and jumped the waist-high, chain-link fence to the backyard in one running jump, like a gymnast going over a pommel horse sideways. At that moment, Ed would later tell me, an athlete was born.

I had tried some sports growing up, like figure skating and soccer, but none had stuck. The missing piece was a father figure's attention, guidance, and support. Ed thought I was special from the start, a feeling I didn't know yet. And honestly, I was nine; what did I know? But I hadn't had a father figure ever, and I had two missing dads: Gordon and bio-dad. Ed had this habit of bringing gifts over when he'd take my mom out on dates. Usually, it was something from the gas station or CVS when he picked up his cigarettes, but I didn't care. It made me feel like a million bucks, and the thoughtfulness made me feel special. I felt seen, valued, and heard because he would get down on one knee and talk to me like a real person. He never treated me like a kid who could be seen and not heard.

Immediately, he got me involved in basketball, and it was the first sport I enjoyed. I loved the time with him and found joy in my athletic ability, which was previously unknown to me. He was the team coach, and it felt good to have both my mom and Ed there at the games. I joined a softball team too. I went from being a small, quiet child to one who started to step into herself.

Ed is a paramount figure in my life, and three of the most salient reasons for that are:

1. *He saw me.* He treated me like my opinion mattered to him. He listened to me, showed interest in me, and made me feel important and smart. And I believed him! He made me believe I could do absolutely anything in life and reinforced this with me often. Nothing was more important to him than quality time. He was my biggest cheerleader and my confidant.

2. *He taught me how to see people.* One of his quirks that would prove important in my career was the fact that every day when I'd come home from school, he'd ask me, "Who did you make smile today?" I had to have an answer, so I would make sure I'd have something to tell him. It made me intentional about humor and connection with people. It was a consistent, fun greeting that got me to open up each day and taught me how to see people.

3. *He gave me a roadmap to success.* Ed was my first coach, and he mastered the balance of teaching and letting me explore and learn on my own. He was able to assess my capability in sports and life and react accordingly.

Ed exuded compassion; he welcomed people to bring their whole selves into every aspect of their lives. With Ed's support, attention, and coaching, I finally found a place where I felt comfortable in my skin. He gave me the conditions to thrive. And these attributes and setting this environment are fundamental to heart-centered leadership.

Compassion is all about seeing other people and recognizing their humanity. Who did you make smile today? Were you focused on other people? What actions did you take to recognize your shared humanity with someone? And an equally important question to "Who did you make smile today?" is "Who did you comfort today?" Focusing on others' experiences in this way enables us to become leaders who support and celebrate their team in equal measure and create trust that is essential for any individual or endeavor to thrive.

DEVELOP EMPATHY

To build a culture of compassion, you must normalize its discussion. And part of that is expanding your emotional vocabulary so that you are better able to discuss building a more compassionate culture and set forth specific practices to achieve your desired goals.

That being said, let's look at a word that is frequently used in conjunction with compassion: "empathy." Empathy is the ability to understand and share the feelings of another (Oxford Dictionary). Empathy requires self-awareness and curiosity about other people and their experiences. We must reflect on our own experiences to fully be present with someone in their feelings.

Reflecting on your experiences, as we talked about in the last chapter, is a helpful exercise for developing empathy. When we connect our feelings to events and events to thought patterns or limiting beliefs, we gain a deeper understanding of ourselves and a bigger capacity for compassion. The more in tune we are with our own emotions and experiences, the better we will be able to observe and discern the feelings and experiences of those around us. You don't have to go through the same experience to lead or respond to people empathetically. It's about understanding what they are feeling and why they are feeling that way.

Every team member in our organization plays an integral role in the company's success, yet it's all too easy for anyone to feel unseen. During the pandemic, many of us had the opportunity to see into our colleagues' whole lives. That's been a wonderful thing. It's a reminder that our team members are so much more than the name that pops up in our Outlook. When we look for ways to engage the people on our team and educate ourselves on the things that are important to them or affecting them, we build empathy into the fabric of our team dynamic.

CELEBRATE DIVERSITY

Businesses need diversity, and diversity thrives on compassion. If you think about it, innovation stems from meeting the diverse needs of those buying your product or service. Your workforce and teams should reflect this diversity to get the broadest and most inclusive solutions. It really is the key to your business success.

The easiest way to attract diverse people is to have diversity in your leadership ranks. We see that crucial talent will no longer accept a workplace that doesn't value and embrace diversity. And it needs to be honest, not just sound pretty. It will become real through mindsets, behaviors, conditions, hiring diverse talent, and listening to their feedback. As leaders, we control all those things with our actions and words. Being a solid and inclusive leader starts with educating yourself on others' experiences and resisting the urge to hire someone modeled after yourself.

Diversity doesn't just refer to gender, race, or ability, though diversity in those areas is critical; it also applies to people who think differently than us or have a different personality style. Embrace those different from you and let them teach you something about themselves, how their minds work, and their cultures.

I've seen and experienced that those who tweak us the hardest have the most to teach us about ourselves. Have you ever noticed that? Usually, when we have a strong reaction to someone, they are reminding us of a part of ourselves we don't like or portraying a behavior we see as a threat to our way of living. The rejection of different limits progress and success. As comfortable as it is living in ignorance, that is not where growth happens. If you want to see growth, you must be willing to get uncomfortable, stretch your ideas, learn from others, and let others teach you.

We can sometimes focus on only the differences we have with people, even if there are some similarities. When we operate this way, it only creates separation. For heart-centered leadership to work, we need to value our differences with others and welcome them into our lives, and as we do, our empathy and compassion will grow. We will learn to love people for who they are in their hearts and how they make us feel. All the other judgments based on fear and societal pressure will fall away.

LEADERSHIP TIP

Diversity can only thrive in an environment rooted in empathy, inclusion, and compassion. To continue your growth as a leader, seek to understand the viewpoints and context of your peers and those above you. Learn what makes them successful and what obstacles they may have. Know your business better than anyone else. Figure out who may block you or get in the way and ensure you understand their context as well. The key to influence is knowledge and curiosity—knowledge of how to motivate people and curiosity about what others are experiencing and how you can invite them into the discussion.

My lessons in diversity started in college. I played four years of softball at the University of Virginia. I was very grateful to get an excellent education at a phenomenal school and play the sport I loved. I started all four years and flourished there. Playing a sport made me feel like I had immediate belonging, so going off to college was not stressful. What I remember most from college was learning about people—people from different parts of the U.S., different socio-economic levels, and different sexual orientations. This experience started my awakening to inclusion outside my own life. I was beginning to understand that society can be cruel to those who don't fit a mold. I'm sure I knew this a bit in high school, but only to a certain extent. Nevertheless, this awakening had a lasting impact on my life and career. I now take on roles in my workplace to ensure inclusion, like being a PRIDE sponsor, and I love making people feel included.

Corporations have systems, and there are intrinsic and extrinsic ways to belong. Don't abandon yourself if you are different. Differences drive change and better ideas. As a leader, don't always default to hiring those like you. Hire those who think differently, who have different experiences and can change the dynamic.

BUILD A SAFE ENVIRONMENT

The best leaders take the time to know their people and remember aspects of their lives. Work is not all about completing tasks. It is also about welcoming the whole person to the team so they can feel safe and seen.

If you care about your people, if they feel valued, respected, and seen, they're going to want to take that tough challenge for you. They're going to want to have your back. They're going to want to put in the extra hours because they feel that you care about them.

A safe environment is built on trust. It is built on creating psychological safety for people to be vulnerable and share their stories. Remember to take time to focus on trust-building with your teams. Taking that extra time will help you navigate challenging times, grueling assignments, and conflict. I've always subscribed to the belief that trust is built on three factors: dependability, capability, and motivation, especially in work.

1. To be trusted, you must be **dependable** and do what you say you will do when you say you will do it. You must deliver or learn how to recontract in advance.

2. You must be **capable**, as well, to see it through to the finish line. You can be the nicest person, but if you don't have the capabilities to do your role, it will be hard for anyone to trust the end product.

3. Finally, to be trusted, your **motivations** need to be clear. Take time to give context to your requests and processes. When people understand your motivations, it will be easier to trust you.

Sharing your motivations is where most people get tripped up, but it is the most significant opportunity for heart-centered leadership. This aspect focuses on sharing your why for deeper understanding and taking the time to understand others' motivations. The easiest way to share your motivations is to provide context to what you do. Why do you do the things you do the way you do them? So often in our daily lives, we make requests without providing context, and the receiver can misunderstand. It is why emails or texts can sometimes be misinterpreted. Misunderstanding happens more often when we don't properly communicate our motivations.

You must spend time creating a safe environment for every relationship you have. You do this by being truthful and transparent with your team and people in your life, by having their backs, and by protecting their confidences. You will create a safe space by letting your people be 100 percent themselves and not trying to mold them into mini versions of you. People need to feel welcome to share their thoughts and feelings without the fear of retribution or judgment. Use phrases like "judgment-free zone" and leave assessments based on biases in the past. In chapter 7, we will discuss an example from a season of my career when I experienced an unsafe psychological environment under a leader who instilled fear and insecurity. This is the antithesis of good leadership. Without compassion and security, employees cannot thrive. Psychological safety is essential to creating high-performing teams and interpersonal relationships. The environment must feel safe.

***

STEEL BACKBONE, SOFT HEART

Compassion is all about looking to others and seeing their needs. Heart-centered leaders embrace compassion as a value and practice it through genuinely seeing others, empathetically communicating, celebrating diversity, and fostering a safe environment for their teams.

Self-compassion is practiced very similarly, but we direct the practices toward ourselves. Look within and reflect on your needs. Consider your experiences and how they made you feel. Celebrate how you are different from the people around you and consider how those differences can better the world and serve to unite teams. And finally, build a home environment that is a safe place to unwind and reflect. Practicing compassion and self-compassion is a revolutionary act in our culture, and with each action we take toward those values, compassion becomes more and more normalized. And our world is in desperate need of compassion as the norm.

COMPASSION

Steel Backbone:
Compassion in the workplace may seem like too soft of a concept, but I encourage you to consider how compassion increases retention and productivity on teams. When you build an environment where people feel supported, they will thrive and be there when you need them most.

What is one way you can help build a more compassionate environment for your team? Think of a weekly activity you could do to foster compassion.

Soft Heart:
The gift of genuinely supporting someone you love and listening to them, not to respond but to understand them, is one of love's greatest gifts. We all want to be seen and valued, whether by a parent, coworker, friend, or lover.

When was the last time you felt truly seen by someone in your life? How can you return the favor to them or someone else?

CHAPTER 3

APPROACHABILITY

Invite Feedback

Some people's picture of leadership looks like a figure who sits up in an ivory tower, or more likely, a corner office in a skyrise. Aloof, detached, above. This is not necessarily an inaccurate picture. While I think plenty of leaders fit this description, it is not true in all cases, and I hope we as a society move toward leadership being associated with a different picture.

Heart-centered leadership is about moving away from a detached way of leading and toward an open, honest, and transparent leadership approach. Heart-centered leadership cares about the company's individual hearts and welcomes professional feedback and suggestions on improving and innovating systems; it is open to different perspectives and is interested in new ways of doing things that would work better for the team overall.

Being approachable is an important trait to develop to be the best leader and self. When I think of approachability, I think of "The Emperor's New Clothes" folktale. If you haven't heard it or need a refresher, basically, two swindlers show up to the capital city to con the Emperor. The Emperor is known for being vain and using the state's money to buy expensive clothes and other material possessions for himself. The conmen present themselves as weavers and offer to make the Emperor magnificent clothes that they claim are invisible to those who are incompetent. When the weavers announce the suit is complete, neither the Emperor nor any of his officials comment on the fact that there is no suit, fearing that others will see them as foolish or incompetent. So the Emperor goes on a procession throughout the whole city in his "new clothes."[5]

I never want to be a leader who looks foolish for fear of looking foolish. The solution to this starts with approachability. I want my team and mentors to feel comfortable coming to me if they see issues with something I've done or said. I want to be a leader aware of the team's realities, problems, and perspectives. This is the only way to grow as an individual and as a team.

Being approachable is not always a natural skill. However, if this is something you want to work on, there are a few ways to address it. The first is to find a really good mentor who will help you recognize your blind spots and challenge your way of thinking. The second is to become a better active listener. Approachability starts with approaching others and seeking their feedback and guidance.

SEEK OUT MENTORS

How do you find a good mentor? The key is to find people who help unlock the real you, people who see you and meet you where you are. Find people who help you untell the parts of your story that are untrue, unfair, and don't serve you. If you are anything like me, you've made the most out of the stories you tell yourself and have turned them into success and significance. You might even be afraid to untell those stories for fear that you might lose drive. But let me tell you, what you gain from telling yourself those stories is not worth the toll it takes on your self-worth.

When finding a mentor, think about what skill, trait, or capability you are trying to enhance. Who do you know who does it expertly? Make a list and reach out to those people. Most people are flattered to be asked. I've had people say to me, "I didn't think I was important enough to ask you." People often miss that most people enjoy being recognized for their expertise.

My 21-year-old daughter, an intern, just practiced this with the president of Merrill Lynch. She sent an email to the president and asked to set up some time to learn from her. Though the president was traveling in Asia and time zones were a challenge, the president linked her with a senior vice president in Nashville who she felt could spend time with her. Even if you get a no, it may come with a suggestion. Sorry for the proud mom brag—but if my young daughter can do this, you can too!

I began receiving executive coaching in April 2010. While I had been in HR communications for years, I had never actually held a proper HR role. My sponsors at Mars felt I'd be good in HR, and like most of the roles in my life, I said, "Why not?" and dove into it. However, it was fraught with peril, as it was an extremely visible position, with the predecessor being in the role for twenty-four years, and it was in the corporate headquarters, partnering with the most senior leaders in Mars. My boss, Aileen, knew I'd need some transition coaching, and we selected Helen-Jane Nelson (HJ).

HJ began by helping me unlock the real person that was buried beneath expectations and who I thought I needed to be. She helped me "untell" my story because the story I had created about myself was very critical and harsh. I had been running from vulnerability like it was a raging fire. I couldn't take failing and tried to hide from being rejected. I was so hypercritical that I never needed anyone to point out my faults. I would beat myself up until my mind could focus on some other aspect of what I needed to do to be loved. Luckily, however, because I was so driven to succeed, I believed in my ability to win—this helped me surpass the fear of rejection that typically comes from trying new things. But it couldn't save me from the years of self-criticism that dominated my personal life.

HJ and I started to focus more on my life's purpose and living intentionally. She helped me see myself and believe there was greatness in me. She helped me see my perceived flaws as gifts. Her most significant gift to me was helping me to find validation within myself. Before this, I needed that acknowledgment from others. This gift set me free! She helped me build my leadership brand: courageous, action-oriented, vulnerable, visionary, creative. She helped me locate my blind spots and shape my leadership story, and I am forever grateful.

To be mentored, you have to be approachable, teachable, and

open-minded. You need to listen with courage and accept feedback with humility. And you need to be able to understand that your mentor's feedback, support, and encouragement come from a place of genuine care. This will enable you to grow into the heart-centered leader you were meant to become.

LEADERSHIP TIP

Are you a leader who wants to be a mentor? Here are the fundamentals to being a good one:

1. Create time and space from the pace of business for a dialogue that results in reflection, learning, and action.

2. Identify shared goals from the mentoring. Help your mentee set career goals to strive toward.

3. Learn more about your mentee's leadership skills and opportunities.

4. Create a business impact statement. Think about what impact your mentee wants to have in their work relationships.

5. Coach the mentee to a personal vision statement and purpose.

6. Commit to the time and prioritize the sessions.

7. Give and receive feedback. Make it mutual.

LOCATE BLIND SPOTS

To make sure we are not blind to our weaknesses, capabilities, and limitations, we need people around us who can be honest with us without fear of negative consequences. We need advisors who will be forthright about how we look in "new clothes," whether that means telling you your lack of punctuality affects your team, your presentation lacks structure, or you would benefit from being friendlier in the office.

Often, we need others to help us truly see what we can't. Unfortunately, most of us spend most of our lives trying to cover over perceived areas of weakness and hurts from the past. Usually, this results in us armoring up and turning down any area of vulnerability, leading to others finding us unapproachable.

While working with HJ, I completed an EQ (Emotional Intelligence) assessment toward the beginning of our coaching experience. While I had an overall high EQ because I had forced myself to be self-aware for protection, one of the shocking results was feedback from others that said they felt like they didn't really know me. I had always thought of myself as very outgoing and personable, so this was a surprise. I was genuinely shocked, but the data was right in front of me. My decisions from those early parts of my life would make me swallow who I was to put on a show of who I thought people wanted me to be. I was masking my true self.

So HJ and I started to work on me. At the time, I was blissfully unaware of how armored I truly was. I thought I was open, but I could not have been further from it. This was my first significant insight: that in my desire to belong and stay safe, I became who I thought people expected me to be. I thought building trust was agreeing with people and that I couldn't dare show any failure.

I worked hard to address perfectionism because that was the first most apparent thing to work on. I had driven myself so hard for so long because I thought being perfect meant being loved. And I couldn't risk being expelled from my family again. So I spent my life crafting an image of who I thought people wanted me to be. I would figure out what my bosses wanted, and I would deliver that and more. I was always a team player; I was able to adapt and adjust to each team I was on. And I believed at my core that I would succeed, because I had to. But while this strategy led to success in the corporate world, it took a toll on me.

During this time with HJ, I was invited to be truly reflective and discover who I was behind the façade. We spent time on my leadership purpose to inspire, develop, and motivate courageous leaders. And she helped me to remove my self-limiting beliefs. I didn't even know I had these beliefs, but once we identified them, there was no going back. It is funny to think about now. I was supremely confident in my intelligence, my ability to be great at jobs, but I was woefully insecure in my belief that I was lovable and worthy. It is very hard to live in those two spaces. I thought I was confident, but my relationships did not corroborate this image.

We spent time learning about systemic coaching, an approach to coaching that "coaches the individual client or team with the system in mind—exploring the part in the whole, and the whole in the part—so as to unlock the potential and performance of both."[6] I learned how to identify and disentangle my feelings from the unresolved issues of previous generations so that I could learn to love who I was versus hate how I came into this world. I had so much to let go of, including a lifetime of shame over being unwanted. And I learned to integrate that thinking into business coaching because every one of us comes from a family, and a corporation is often rooted in a family system.

The feedback I received from others during this time was invaluable to my professional and personal growth. I was thankful for people who pointed out my blind spots to me; otherwise, I would never have known I needed to work on them, and blind spots would have hindered me from stepping into and being my whole self.

Look for patterns in your life. What lessons and experiences seem to repeat? Like dating different people and having the same experience with all of them. Or the same experience over and over with a different boss or employer. Usually, there is a common denominator of an experience you are meant to learn. For example, one of mine was not using my voice when I felt insecure. Once I could see and break this pattern, I became a new person.

Everyone has blind spots, and they are called blind spots for a reason. These blind spots can impede our approachability. We need the people around us to tell us what they are. If you are unwilling to listen, to swallow your pride for a second and ask for feedback on what you can do better, you will keep on living and leading without full vision. It's time to stop hindering yourself and ignoring the obvious. Instead, reach out for honest feedback from those around you on areas you could improve and move forward with greater clarity.

INVITE CHALLENGE

When you're approachable and invite feedback, people will challenge you. They will challenge the way you think, and they will challenge you to become a better version of yourself. You must be strong to accept the challenge and malleable to change for the better.

HJ introduced me to another coach, Judy Smith, a family dynamics specialist. With Judy, I was going to explore my beliefs about my adoption and its impact on me. In life, you have to attack the proverbial monsters under your bed, and this was mine.

Being an adoptive mom herself, Judy helped me feel safe in sharing my experiences because she came from some level of understanding of the adoption process. As you start exploring your past, it is important to find someone you can talk with where you feel safe. Judy helped me disentangle my subconscious thoughts about myself and put them in their proper place. This exercise made me realize I didn't need to carry the shame that my biological mother undoubtedly felt when she was shipped out of her house for carrying me in her womb. I realized I had been assuming that burden, and that posture of shame made me play small when I felt at risk.

Judy taught me how to be comfortable with my origin, who I was, and how I showed up in this world. She taught me about being intentional and manifesting. These are things I just wasn't aware of. Now the words "intentional" and "manifesting" seem like household terms, and even my fifteen-year-old talks about manifesting (she learned it on TikTok). However, at the time, it was all new to me.

In my two years with Judy, I learned incredible things about adoptees and the deeper wounds that can stem from adoption. Judy helped me release the burdens I was carrying and give those bad thoughts their place, which was not in my psyche. It was a transformational experience.

I'll never forget when Judy asked me, "How big do you want to be?" It was a foundational question and one I had never thought of. I was genuinely motivated to succeed but never really had an endpoint. I share this with you as I know she'd like you to answer this question for yourself. Think big, turn failures into triumphs, and take your place in this life.

If we are never challenged, we will never grow. Finding safety in our comfort zones and current leadership styles may limit our professional and personal relationships. When we find people who challenge our thinking and help us dig deeper into our current thought lives, we will grow in how we connect and interact with others. By showing we are not afraid to be challenged, we become more approachable to the people around us.

LISTEN WELL

I've noticed throughout my career that many leaders have active listening on their development plan. Many of us were never taught how to listen. They call it "active" listening because you have to pause and listen to understand what someone is saying. Most people listen to respond, which can look like a ping pong game of one-ups-manship. We have all been in those conversations. "Oh yeah, something similar happened to me but way worse . . ."

Listening to understand requires empathy and heart because not only are you listening to the words, but you are also listening to the meaning behind the words and the energy surrounding the words. I like to draw on Maya Angelou's famous quote "People will forget what you say, but they will never forget the way you make them feel." Listening to understand creates a mutual appreciation between the speaker and listener. You know when this happens because you can feel the person genuinely tuning in to what you are saying without an agenda or impatience.

Listening is a crucial attribute to approachability and a core part of the model of learning agility, which effectively assesses the potential of a leader or individual. This model is called

Lominger's Learning Agility Architect™, and it is an assessment to measure learning agility across five factors: self-awareness, mental agility, change agility, people agility, and results agility. It provides individuals with a methodology to develop and enhance their learning agility and support their career growth. In the Self-Awareness and People Agility categories, you will find that listening is an important core attribute to fulfilling your potential. You can be smart and deliver, but you won't reach your full potential if you don't understand how to inspire, motivate, and develop people.[7]

When we listen well, we begin to understand people's motivations, expectations, and communication styles. This enables us to approach people and situations in the most effective way possible. When we listen well, we treat people as individuals with unique needs, strengths, and insights, making others feel they can approach us and be seen and heard. Your ability to listen is fundamental to others viewing you as approachable.

***

HJ and Judy helped me identify a stronger leadership stance and presence, but equally as important, they helped me see and appreciate the true me. I'm thankful to have found mentors who cared enough to work with me until I became a more developed, evolved person, thus developing me into a better leader for others.

Perfection is not a standard anyone can be held to or successfully live up to. When we finally let go of the façade of a perfect person, we immediately become more relatable and approachable. We all have limitations and areas that need improvement, but the key is how we frame it. Do we see areas of improvement as shameful and to be avoided and downplayed? Or do we see them as opportunities for growth and to reach our potential? We all have an infinite capacity for growth, but we can only achieve it when we open ourselves up and invite others to approach us with feedback.

APPROACHABILITY

Steel Backbone:

An important aspect of being a great leader is ensuring that people feel comfortable coming to you with feedback, ideas, and suggestions. The way you interact with people and lead meetings will give your team a sense of how approachable you are.

What are ways that you can increase your approachability and invite more feedback?

Soft Heart:

One thing that helps increase our approachability is how we approach others. When we compassionately relay feedback and use it as an opportunity to inspire and encourage people, we communicate our approachability.

The next time you give someone feedback, stop and think of ways to communicate it compassionately.

CHAPTER 4

INTENTIONALITY

Balance Your Priorities Through Setting Boundaries

Intentionality is what turns dreamers into leaders. Intentionality is what strengthens backbones and softens hearts. To be successful heart-centered leaders, we need to be intentional about integrating our values into all aspects of our lives and setting proper boundaries to balance our priorities.

When we aren't specific about our priorities and values, we'll often find ourselves off course. Life has a way of turning us around, shaking us up, and spitting us out. Going through life without clear priorities is like driving into a hurricane and expecting to end up at your destination—it doesn't quite work out. We need a map and a game plan to navigate what life throws our way.

Clearly defining our priorities and core values helps guide our major decisions, especially when it comes to work and leadership. When we are clear with ourselves and others about our priorities, it becomes easier to set boundaries that help us keep our priorities and values at the core of our work and relationships.

MAKING YOUR MAP

As leaders, it is important to constantly evaluate where we are going and leading others. If we want to celebrate the humanity of our teams, then we need to lead by example by pursuing a balanced life. We can do this by mapping out our priorities and core values and keeping an eye on them to make sure we are giving every priority and value the time and weight they are due. If any single priority is getting all our attention or if we aren't practicing one of our values, that means we've lost sight of the whole person and are only focusing on one aspect.

PRIORITY EXERCISE

Determine your five top priorities by reflecting on what is most important to you in life.

My priorities are:

1. Family

2. Spirituality

3. Friends

4. Work

5. Hobbies and personal care

Each of your priorities needs time and attention for you to thrive and be the best possible leader. This doesn't mean that each priority gets an equal amount of time; it just means finding the right balance so that you feel rested and fulfilled. Some of your priorities have specific time requirements. You must be strategic about the pockets of time you have to ensure all your priorities are accounted for.

Working a forty-to-fifty-hour week means there is less time for self-care and hobbies, but maybe five hours of personal reading per week is all that is needed for you to feel fulfilled in that area of your life. Balance is less about equality when it comes to priorities and more about managing your time in a way that works for you and your schedule.

CORE VALUES EXERCISE

Determine your top five core values by thinking of traits that define you or traits that represent who you are when you're at your best.

My core values are:
1. Learning and growing
2. Courage
3. Adventure
4. Creativity
5. Fun

Your core values are the guiding lights that lead you through difficult times and hard decisions. When we intentionally incorporate these values into all aspects of our lives, we will see a massive difference in our happiness, fulfillment, and growth. Once you figure out what your core values are, you can then analyze how they are present in your life, love, and leadership and where are they are lacking.

Knowing my values helped me understand why I would feel out of sorts with certain people's behaviors and why certain situations made me uncomfortable. For example, I loved being in HR but couldn't explain why something felt missing in my life. I learned from this lesson that I had a deep need for creativity, which was missing in my HR role, but I got to experience it more through my prior roles in marketing and communications. I was so used to tapping into that creative part of my brain, and I loved when I felt "in flow." However, the absence of this became very palpable, and I needed to find a way to work it back into my life. So, I turned this revelation into a new way to tap into creativity in my life—my love for cooking.

Prior to this experiment, I looked at cooking as a chore. However, with this new insight, I threw myself into learning how to be a really good cook with my usual zest for new things. This search to put creativity back into my life spawned a love for cooking for people and entertaining. Now, the kitchen is my sanctuary. This experiment allowed me to settle into my HR role more deeply and find an outlet that genuinely nourished my soul. Sometimes we need to learn that our partner or job can't fulfill all our needs, which is okay. We can learn to supplement those needs and give the other areas in our life the purpose they are intended to fill.

Writing my values down was also important because I finally recognized the value of courage. It was this revelation that made me look at how courageous I had been my entire life without giving it the proper acknowledgment. I had been kicking myself so hard for every mistake I made that I missed all the bravery in my story. I began to realize how special I was. I started to see that life is about taking courageous steps to overcome challenges and then telling those stories so others can benefit. It is how I am here writing this book today!

The simple task of writing down your values and priorities can shift your work happiness, help you discover a new outlet to relieve stress, and help you appreciate the forgotten parts of who you are—from simple things to great insights. Take the time and do the work. Knowing who you are, what you most connect with, and what you want to achieve can help form your life's purpose.

SETTING YOUR BOUNDARIES

When you get intentional and clear about your priorities and values, you will find that when you make requests, the world aligns around you to make them happen. Have you ever noticed that when you are clear on a goal, you start to see more possibilities to help you achieve it? When we don't have that clarity, our eyes are not fully open to the opportunities before us.

When you are intentional about your boundaries, you create the space to find more balance in your life, enabling you to bring your priorities and values to life. What are the right boundaries? Only you will know; however, they will revolve around the people, beliefs, and focus we all need to feel valued, respected, loved, and purposeful.

For me, family dinners have always been a critical boundary and important value I want to uphold. I grew up with homemade family dinners every night, cooked by my mother or grandmother. I cherish these memories, and I want to create them for my children. So, throughout my career, I've made it known that I am an early starter so I can get home in time each day to have dinner with my family. Balance for me means not sacrificing key moments with my family because of work. I don't mind putting in the hours later, but those few hours with my family in the evening are sacred and help me feel balanced.

To live a balanced life, you may need to switch careers or companies. You may just need to be more specific and organized when setting your calendar for the month. It may mean you need to wake up thirty minutes earlier in the morning so you can start your day with a calming activity. Balance means and requires different things from different people. Evaluate how balanced you feel in your life right now and begin exploring ways to achieve greater balance in your daily life.

LEADERSHIP TIP

Spend time getting very precise about what you want and then live your life as if you already have it.

If you're in a new role or simply looking for better balance in the one you have, here's my advice for being intentional about what's important to you:

1. **Ask about expectations and make your boundaries clear.**

Ask your boss to be clear when something is urgent or can wait. When I began working in the Mars headquarters, I quickly realized that most people worked from 7:00 a.m. to 7:00 p.m. It was a global business, and we had to be accessible to other time zones. I knew that would present a challenge for me because of family dinner. I had a boss who came to work at 5:30 a.m. and left at 7:30 p.m., and I could have tried to emulate that to make a good impression. However, being very clear in my family goals, I started that job with a clear mission to make it okay to work and have a life.

I discussed this with my boss from the angle of coming from my heart rather than demanding something different. She took the time to understand my needs and how we could work together to set me up for success. She was completely supportive. Her support made it possible, yet I still needed the courage to ask.

At the first all-associate communication meeting at Mars, I shared my story and my beliefs. I also communicated clearly how my working hours might be different, but it didn't mean I wasn't working. It merely meant I took a break from 5:00-9:00 p.m. to be with my family. I chose to work a "second shift" from 9:00-11:00 p.m. to ensure I played by the same rules as everyone else. For me, making dinner and being present with my family lit me up. To others, it started to change the narrative of a one-size-of-working-fits-all mentality. Together we began to embrace different ways of working.

Your manager's expectations don't nullify your boundaries. Get creative and find ways to set clear boundaries and meet your manager's expectations. If the way the company currently runs things isn't effective and doesn't lend itself to a balanced life, approach your manager and discuss the goals and a more productive and effective solution.

And if you are the one setting expectations for someone else, make sure you communicate what is expected and why it's expected. The key to avoiding getting "upset" over unmet expectations is to "set up" clear expectations with people, whether in your personal or professional life.

As individuals, we have firm expectations of how people treat us: how quickly they respond to us, what considerations they give us, what share of time in their life we get. We often skip telling them our expectations, leaving them ignorant of the rules of engagement.

Many people are afraid to share their expectations because they feel they will be rejected, laughed at, or be in a space that feels too vulnerable. When we don't share our expectations, we get upset with that person, and our joy is diminished.

People and employees are not mind readers. Set clear expectations and share the rationale behind the ask. Expectations with context and alignment will drive the right environment for success and joy to blossom.

2. Deliver where it counts.

What is most important for your career and your company is playing your role and helping the business grow. If you're a good performer, your boundaries are just part of the package.

It's funny how patterns follow you. When I left Mars to go to SmileDirectClub, the business was a young startup growing at hyper speed and had a "25/8" culture to keep up with the growing demand, meaning you didn't just work 24/7. It was 25/8 at SDC, and it was very much an "in-person" place of employment. This scared me a little, but I am always up for a challenge, and this seemed like a worthy one. I negotiated early on that I could be away from the office for soccer games and kid events. I was very clear they would get great productivity out of me if I could have these moments that matter. They said yes, as did I, and the entire leadership team at SDC slowly began to replace the 25/8 culture with a more balanced work environment. We have changed this now entirely at SDC; kudos to my CEO and COO for recognizing this was the right path for us and supporting this evolution along the way. Sometimes there are cultural elements that seem sacred. Have the courage to take them on. Sometimes the myth is more significant than the business value. Have data, present a case, and make meaningful change.

3. **Fiercely advocate for your boundaries because if you don't respect them, no one else will either.**

There were many times I was asked to join a late meeting or moments when I could have chosen to stay late to finish something; however, I would have then been violating my boundaries. So, I would respectfully ask if the meeting could be at a different time. I never minded an early morning meeting to counter my dinner. And I realized that if people saw me staying late, it would confuse the message I had openly shared. I certainly had to make some choices that conflicted with my dinner value, but I made those decisions with intentionality and purpose rather than feeling pressured to do so.

Advocating for your boundaries can be difficult at times, and this is why clearly defining your values and priorities is so important. Use them as a map for setting your boundaries and enforcing them. Write them down, put them on a sticky note you keep on your desk, and keep them front and center so that you can lead and set boundaries with intentionality.

4. Talk openly with your colleagues about balance and boundaries.

We often feel we are the only ones struggling with an issue. When you start talking about your struggles and challenges, you invite others to help you think about the situation. I recently saw this transform a whole organization struggling with work/life balance. It was as simple as a Town Hall where each leader shared what they do to protect their work/life balance. The transparency and honesty helped people see that defining your work/life balance is a priority for leadership, and it showed them it is okay to do that for themselves. Hearing leaders voice something like this permits others to do so as well.

If you're looking for acceptance of the boundaries you set, make sure you support those set by the people around you. Be the change you want to see. Talk openly about boundary setting. Be the champion for these types of discussions and take the time to acknowledge others who do it well. For movements to happen, you need a first follower, and then you can create a community that really drives change.

5. Reward yourself for sticking to your boundaries.

Standing up for yourself can be one of the most challenging paths.

It is all too easy to sacrifice our values because we think we will please others by saying yes. When you stay true to yourself and get through a tough challenge, reward yourself to mark the win. We like cupcakes in our house!

* * *

When we are intentional about how we live, love, and lead, we will find more of the elusive balance we are always looking for. Determine your priorities and core values, as these will be your map for making decisions and setting boundaries in the future. Once you have your map, you'll be able to navigate setting boundaries with clarity, confidence, and conviction. This level of intentionality is a game-changer as you seek to lead with a steel backbone and soft heart.

INTENTIONALITY

Steel Backbone:

Being intentional about boundaries is crucial to living a fulfilling, well-rounded life and not becoming a victim of burnout. Setting personal boundaries is beneficial in your relationships and friendships because it allows you to maintain a healthy level of dependency and take care of yourself.

What is an area in your professional or personal life where you think setting a clearer boundary would enable you to thrive? Intentionally set those boundaries, not just internally but externally—make them known to the people who need to know.

Soft Heart:

Intentionality when it comes to our core values enables us to take inventory of our lives and assess if there is anything we can do to better care for ourselves and create conditions to thrive.

What is a core value you've been neglecting that you can focus on this week? How can you build activities that encourage your core beliefs into your schedule?

CHAPTER 5

INCLUSION

Foster a Culture of Belonging

How do I fit in? Will I be accepted for me? Will I be rejected? These questions have plagued us all at some point. The desire to feel included, valued, and heard is something we share, and we can all probably recall moments when we felt left out. Do you remember the fear of walking into the lunchroom on the first day of middle school? To which table did you "belong"? Maybe you remember waiting to be picked for the sports team in gym, praying not to be the last one chosen. These are visceral memories for many. Starting a new job can evoke these feelings as well. This desire to fit in rings true in the workplace, and it's our job as leaders to help foster a culture of belonging, where everyone can bring their full selves to work—one big table for all.

While this mindset may seem simple, bringing it to life in a constantly changing and evolving workplace requires dedication. We all need to belong. It is the cornerstone of an effective retention strategy. When we are dedicated to our team, they, in turn, will stay dedicated to us.

Being inclusive is also essential in our personal lives. Whether you have a partner and children or want to start a family one day, being inclusive of other styles is essential to ensuring that everyone in your corner feels that they belong. As leaders of teams and families, fostering an environment where everyone feels they have a seat at the table and a voice worthy of being heard is essential to leading with a steel backbone and soft heart. The table is usually where the best ideas and most meaningful memories are created, so make sure there are enough chairs for everyone.

WE'RE ALL FAMILY HERE

Many workplaces describe the work environment as a family. And while they are trying to communicate the loyalty and closeness of the team, most of the time, the reality is more akin to dysfunctional Thanksgiving gatherings with uncles you talk to twice a year. But I think healthy work environments where heart-centered leadership is practiced do reflect the spirit of closeness and loyalty seen in healthy family dynamics.

My marriage and children have taught me much about the inclusion required to be a great leader. I met Jack in 1994 and was drawn to how sweet he was. My relationship with Jack was the first one that felt genuinely mutual. Jack appreciated my uniqueness and made me feel safe. When I met Jack, I was ready for something real, and I wanted to be with someone who would support me and never leave me. We got engaged in the fall of 1996 and got married in 1997.

Coming into this relationship, I had fervently carried around the limiting belief that I wasn't worthy, deserving, or capable of being loved. This feeling drove me to try to "win" love from people and to rely on work success as the only way to feel good about myself. However, it was incredibly exhausting and depleting. When I got married, I felt this burden, this heavy weight, lighten. I could put down a huge limiting belief and could finally just be me. My foundation shifted into place. And together, we started building our family.

My oldest daughter, Marlena, was born on March 3, 2000. She came bounding into our lives with the force that she remains today. Marlie's birth introduced to me my first blood relative, and I wasn't sure if I would have a momentous shift in my being. All I know is that her birth felt miraculous to me, and I loved her beyond any human description. I recall being relieved because I believed my mom, Jan, felt about me the way I felt about Marlie. I had always wondered if there was a difference between biological and adoptive children. My felt experience is that strong parental love extends beyond blood and that I belonged just for being who I am.

Our second, Jessie, was born on October 3, 2003. She came into this world as a quiet, easy baby. She was and is very reflective and more reserved. We used to say she looked so serious as a baby, but she quickly turned into a silly, mischievous, and sweet little girl. Everything was easier the second time around, and I was so much more comfortable. Isn't this true of all things? Once we see an arc all the way through, we can recognize it and feel more comfortable the second time. And she was such an easy baby, so sweet. I enjoyed my maternity leave with her and savored every moment because I thought she was our last baby.

When I was pregnant with Jessie, I just knew she would have that athletic side of me. It felt destined, and she did indeed become an accomplished athlete in her own right. We gave her my birth certificate middle name, Ann, as a way to carry forward the innocence and wonder of my youth. This shared identity was just one aspect of the love and gifts I wanted to bestow on her.

I had two miscarriages after Jessie was born. I will never forget going to the doctor for a check-up in 2004 and being told my baby didn't have a heartbeat. It was the most horrible, gut-wrenching thing I had ever experienced. I was devastated. For someone who was an athlete and used to her body being one of her most vital attributes, this felt like a huge betrayal. I went back and forth in blaming myself and blaming my body.

I had warmed up to the idea of a third child. The miscarriage set off a deep sorrow that I had never experienced before. And it made me want another child with a fierceness I didn't expect. I had been fortunate thus far in my life, and this seemed like an error. It was my first actual loss of innocence and my first brush with death. Jack was not sure how to help me, and our relationship floundered a bit.

When I got pregnant again in 2005, I was happy and optimistic. However, in December, I started bleeding on the day before my birthday. I went to the doctor and got the terrible news again. If my first miscarriage shocked and stunned me, this one was a knock-out blow. I felt like I had failed these babies. The pain felt so heavy. I took the blame, figuring I must be doing something wrong. It was debilitating for someone so attached to control, and it was even more devastating the second time around. I was broken, in pain, and felt very alone. Failure can feel this way if we don't give it a purpose.

I felt as if something I did made this happen. I became fixated on learning more about why I miscarried. It became a quest. My doctor suggested I get some genetic testing, given I was adopted, and I discovered I had something called MTHFR—you can look up the very long name of this abbreviation. I used to call it Mother Fucker. It was a genetic mutation that made me more prone to blood clots, and it gave me a reason why I had miscarried. Yet I remained determined. So, I set off again, with my belief in God, my sheer determination, and a life I knew was meant to find me.

And so, we became pregnant again in March 2006. This pregnancy went much better, and my doctors more closely supervised me. Based on my past miscarriages, I had to take baby aspirin and testosterone to help "hold the pregnancy." Whatever we did worked because Ava was born on December 19, 2006. She came into this world perfect and with a wonderful message: you can let failure topple you, or you can keep fighting. This lesson would prove to be foundational for later events in my life.

During my miscarriages, I felt so alone and was unsure I could forgive myself if I couldn't right these wrongs. This new realization—that I was vulnerable and that life is vulnerable—scared me. At this moment, my old survival skills of fight or flight kicked in. I chose to fight even though I kept losing. I chose to fight even though I risked more loss. And I did so because I had a purpose. I knew I was meant to have Ava. She came out strong, born one day after my birthday, with a powerful resemblance to her mother. I had never looked like anyone, but now I had this little mini-me. All of my children have a piece of my soul in various ways. Ava's gift to me is to remind me of that little girl I used to be who faced life with optimism. I needed that back.

I faced devastating times with my family, times that I didn't always handle well. I can say with certainty that I broke after that second miscarriage. Jack and I were not equipped to support each other, and it created a schism. Looking back, the feeling of brokenness was a big lesson that life is not always fair. I know that sounds a bit juvenile, but it was the first time I realized things may not always go my way.

But the biggest lesson I learned as Jack and I were building a family was the power of acceptance and belonging. When I had my daughters, I was finally on the giving end of the unconditional belonging I wanted as a child—and feeling that strong sense of inclusion changed me forever and changed the way I lead. When we focus on the inclusion and belonging of the people we are responsible for, we create an environment where they can develop steel backbones and soft hearts.

HAVE THEM AT HELLO

Though inclusion is practiced differently in a work setting versus a family setting, the principles and purpose are similar: inclusion communicates the care, acceptance, and belonging essential for anyone to thrive.

Belonging starts at, well, the start. When you are a leader, you cannot undervalue the importance of welcoming new members. They need to know they belong from the beginning. The first day should provide new members with opportunities to listen and learn about the culture and connect to the strategy of the business. As a leader, you can achieve this with a thorough onboarding process that focuses on an individual's purpose, vision, and values. It should highlight the diversity of thought that goes into your brand and establish rules of engagement across the business.

It's important to provide your team with the right connection points, learning opportunities, and the ability to build relationships with peers, leadership, and direct reports. For any roles that involve people leadership, taking that extra step to ensure a sense of team belonging is often the missing piece.

As a leader, you must make time for the moments that matter and talk about life. Every Monday, my team kicks off the week with a coffee date, where we recap our weekends and discuss what's on our minds. It's time we've set aside to connect and bond with one another, and it's honestly one of the highlights of my work week. With a lot of meetings being virtual now, those organic connections don't happen unless you make time for them.

For more in-depth team bonding, consider annual or quarterly team connects. These can create moments that matter in very meaningful ways. I like to hold two meetings per year to review business strategy and bond as a team. Both are equally as important. We will spend a day on business strategy and performance and a day on how we can continue to cultivate a sense of belonging throughout our function and with each other. Nothing drives someone's sense of belonging more than a safe space to share their true selves and all that makes them who they are.

FEWER, BIGGER, BETTER

I have coached many female leaders, and most of them tell me they have to work twice as hard to get that promotion or have had to battle the perception that they aren't as committed because they are moms. I've experienced feeling like I had to work myself to the bone to prove myself. I know the temptation to try to do it all to show your value. But often, by working smarter and not harder, we can do more good while taking better care of ourselves.

"Fewer, bigger, better" is a mantra I frequently share with my teams. At its core, it means that of the 100 things you can focus on, choose to dedicate your time and effort to the few things that have the most impact and make your project, organization, and life better. This is what separates success from martyrdom. You can't be all things to all people. You have to figure out how best to move the ball forward and communicate well to bring along the most people with you. Otherwise, we burn ourselves out trying to do everything.

Consider starting in a new role at a new business. Usually, you will find multiple ways to add value, and it may be challenging to figure out where to start. Some people try to do it all and then do a marginal job at everything because they are stretched too thin. Imagine a leaky pipe that has 20 leaks across it. You can exhaust yourself trying to stop them individually, or you can identify the primary water source and turn off the water. The water stops, and you focused on the one or two avenues that impact the overall problem. Fewer, bigger, better!

You could practice being inclusive with your team in 1,000 different ways, but that doesn't mean you should. Instead, focus on a few key areas that will help foster a culture of belonging and do them really well. This strategy will ultimately have more impact than trying and failing at inclusion in 1,000 different ways.

Being a dedicated leader doesn't mean carrying all the weight. When you don't wear yourself out doing tasks you could easily delegate to other people, you'll have more time and energy to do your required tasks with the utmost excellence. Being dedicated doesn't mean doing everything; it means committing yourself to a few key things so you can do them bigger and better.

SEEK MUTUALITY

During my years at Mars, there was a set of five principles that all associates lived by: quality, responsibility, efficiency, mutuality, and freedom. I personally always loved mutuality because it focused on creating "win-win" relationships. Those years taught me to pause before I communicated what would be the correct answer for me and assess how to make every situation a win-win. When acting from a place of mutuality, you have to expand your perspective outside of your own interests and consider how all can thrive together. Communication based on mutuality is inclusive, motivating, and more impactful because everyone feels part of it.

The key to mutuality is to believe that the shared win will magnify the effectiveness of what you are trying to do. When people feel included and seen, they are more likely to support and perpetuate what you are trying to achieve. I learned a hard lesson on this topic when I was called to address a room full of associates to share that we would be reducing our workforce. As I approached the communication, I had the talking points; however, I was worried about my performance. I was worried about whether I would have the right answers. I was worried that I would forget my talking points. And in all that worry, a very wise associate named Angel said to me, "This is not about you; it is about them. Just focus on what they need to hear and speak from your heart to their hearts." This simple advice invited me to think about how I could make this experience feel more balanced and how they could feel this was not a one-way message. Mutuality is rooted in the systemic principle that there needs to be a balance of giving and receiving in all we do with people. Otherwise, relationships get out of balance, and people can't connect.

Being dedicated to mutuality with your team is important for seeing eye to eye. When you set expectations, but the outcome of those expectations only serves you, your team will likely face burnout and lose trust. But if the expectations you set are clearly communicated and mutually beneficial, your team is likely to work harder and be more loyal.

I've seen this in my relationships with my daughters as well. If one of my daughters asks if she can go to a party on a Friday night, and I say, "No, you can't go. End of discussion," I am not fostering a sense of mutuality. But if I turn her request into a conversation where both voices are being heard, it will more likely result in a win-win situation. If I allow my daughter to explain why she wants to go and who else will be there, she'll be more likely to listen to my concerns and requests. The ultimate answer might be the same, but it's how you arrive at the destination that matters. With mutuality, you can foster a sense of belonging and dedication that deepens connection.

***

Being inclusive starts with leadership. Embrace your role as team uniter; it does not happen on its own. Keep your ears to the ground and focus your eyes on your team. You need to care about what they care about. This is imperative to creating a culture of belonging. Through the pandemic, we learned that our world is constantly evolving, and the workforce, more often than not, will need to evolve too. Be open to new ideas and the pivot. Listen to your team members' needs. Create connections and moments that matter. Learn about the people who make up your organization and honor their individuality—celebrate it too. Make your organization one big lunch table and pull up a seat for everyone.

INCLUSION

Steel Backbone:

Great leaders communicate with clarity and mutuality to achieve the best result for the team or the relationship. It is important to have conviction, stand your ground, and fight for what you believe is the best decision, but it is also important to listen to others' perspectives and have an open, inclusive mind.

When was the last time you had a differing opinion from someone about a decision that needed to be made? How did the situation resolve? Would you do anything differently?

Soft Heart:

Being an inclusive leader can sometimes feel overwhelming because there may be so many viewpoints, and it can be hard to discern the path forward. Adopting a broad perspective makes it easier to focus on a few, bigger, better solutions. Sometimes we need to focus on only a few things and not try to be all things to all people. Inclusion built on doing everything leads to burnout, whereas inclusion built on wise discernment leads to a flourishing team.

Where in your life can you apply the principle of fewer, bigger, better? Where are you doing too much, and how can you scale back?

CHAPTER 6

VULNERABILITY

Let People In

Vulnerability in the workplace may still sound like an oxymoron to you or sound like your worst nightmare, but it is a cornerstone principle of heart-centered leadership. In her book *Daring Greatly*, author and researcher Brené Brown states, "Vulnerability is the core, the heart, the center, of meaningful human experiences." And she defines vulnerability as "uncertainty, risk, and emotional exposure."[8]

Vulnerability allows us to connect with others on a deeper level. Ultimately, it allows us to have a sense of shared humanity with someone. But to do this, we have to let our guards down and let people in, which is always a risk.

Being vulnerable in the workplace is difficult because we've been told our whole lives to be professional, which basically translates to "be as emotionally neutral as possible," but that's not how humans were created to function. Instead, we were created with emotions that inform every aspect of our lives—and that is something to be celebrated and monitored, not diminished.

Toward the beginning of the pandemic, when I would talk with friends and professionals at other companies, I found we were all experiencing some version of this feeling—what psychologists call "anticipatory grief." It's a sense of dread, anxiety, and sadness in the face of the unknown and potential loss. A friend described it to me as "just feeling so unsettled in all aspects."

It was a time of vulnerability—uncertainty, risk, and emotional exposure. All of a sudden, your boss saw your cat scurrying across your living room during a Zoom meeting. Unexpectedly, you were let go of a job you loved. Suddenly, you were unable to see people you saw close to every day in the months leading up to the lockdown. And then everything changed, and we were feeling collective isolation. It was vulnerable.

The most significant difference I noticed between leaders who handled the uncertainty of the beginning of the pandemic well versus those who didn't was the acknowledgment of the uncertainty and vulnerability. Heart-centered leaders made great effort to find ways to connect with their teams, not just to support individuals in their roles but to check in with them on how they were doing and feeling with all that was changing around them. While on the other hand, I noticed that some leaders didn't acknowledge the vulnerability of the situation and pushed their teams to work harder under the new conditions, most likely out of fear that people weren't working hard enough at home. I'll let you guess which leaders retained more of their teams.

Heart-centered leaders acknowledge the humanity of their teams and work to create environments that encourage vulnerability.

There are three practices that will help you exercise vulnerability:

1. Let people in by sharing some of your origin story.

2. Share some of what's currently going on in your life outside of work with someone on your team who you trust.

3. Ask for help.

These are practices you need to incorporate even as a leader. You will set the tone of vulnerability for your team. But something else you can do is initiate those conversations with your team by asking them what is going on in their lives outside of work and following up with them on what they tell you. Encourage them to ask for help and support when they need it.

HOW TO KNOW WHAT TO SHARE

I remember the day my coach HJ asked me to watch a TED Talk by Brené Brown. This was before Brené became a worldwide phenom, and I hadn't heard of her before. I queued it up and thought, *Wow, this is a long one.* But I sat at my desk and watched. What unfolded in front of me brought tears to my eyes. Brené's work on shame and vulnerability was like a beacon to me, and as someone who coaches others, I could immediately see the link to the workplace.

I cried and had to leave my desk and take a walk. What she spoke about was exactly how I felt. I quickly picked up her book *The Gifts of Imperfection* and had the most profound experience. I always thought I felt unworthy and pressed for perfection because of my adoption. Yet by reading this book, I realized many people carry this unhealthy belief. I wasn't alone. The lessons inside *The Gifts of Imperfection* freed me from my past and encouraged me to move through it versus hanging on to some old story. And perhaps more important, it gave me insight into the struggle that so many of us experience.

I remember saying to HJ, "I don't cry, and I know it is not a good thing." It was too vulnerable, and I spent a lifetime hiding my feelings. HJ had a way of helping me let go of all the protections had I put into place and get to the emotions driving my behaviors. I started to learn how to be vulnerable by slowly sharing my story. I had never told people I was adopted, and now I was starting to share with the teams I led at work. I was so afraid to do this. I know it seems easy for most people, but for me, I had subconsciously tied a survival bias to it, and it felt scary.

When it comes to opening up in the workplace, Brené Brown has some excellent advice on what to share and what not to share. She says, "I only share when I have no unmet needs that I'm trying to fill. I firmly believe that being vulnerable with a larger audience is only a good idea if the healing is tied to the sharing, not to the expectations I might have for the response I get."[9] You don't need to tell everyone about everything to foster a sense of vulnerability in the workplace. Have discretion and make sure you're creating a space for people to feel safe.

I recall applying for a job in Nashville at a company with two openings for vice presidents. I didn't get the "big one," but I did get the other one for a smaller part of the business. I remember the president of the larger role telling me he felt more connected to the other candidate and that I was selling myself too much. I took this chance to share my adoption story and how my behaviors sometimes come off that way because I feel I have to prove I belong. I was shaking and so afraid to admit this. He appreciated my vulnerability, and it formed a bond between us that would be helpful later after I moved to Nashville for the job I did get. It felt very risky at the time, but it turned into a massive step forward for me. As it would turn out, that same leader created one regional structure over those two businesses, and he selected me to work with him just one year later.

The lesson here is that vulnerability can be scary, yet with the right resources and support, you can learn how to embrace it. You need to step into your vulnerability. It is your greatest gift to humanity. You will connect better with people, and you will be able to release your shame, fear, and sorrow.

SHARE WITH OTHERS ABOUT WHAT'S GOING ON

I had my first taste of the need for vulnerability when I went through one of the worst times in my life. It was 2010, and I was starting a new job, having very conflicting feelings about my marriage, and coming into my own as a person. I was already unsettled. Then I got the news no one wants. The man who became my present dad and first mentor, Ed Duffy, had been diagnosed with Stage 4 terminal metastatic small cell cancer. Ed had been a lifelong smoker and drinker. My mom was always on him to quit both. The irony of this whole story is that Ed himself had decided to quit smoking. He had just stopped for about four months when he noticed he wasn't feeling well.

The diagnosis was a death sentence. I felt like I had stopped breathing the moment I heard the news. The world was somehow spinning faster, yet I was moving in slow motion with no air. It was hard to comprehend the words, and my brain just wanted to turn off. How could this be? He had just quit smoking, and then this? I felt myself shrink down to that nine-year-old girl who first met him when I was fleeing my brother. He was always there for me when I felt like escaping. He was the first man who stayed in my life and was reliable, dependable, and loving. Why him? I felt like I was being cheated. My daughters at the time were ten, six, and three. Marlie knew him so well, and I also wanted that for my other daughters. It was soul-crushing news that we received a week before Ed's birthday, yet at that moment, I had to put it aside to make his birthday the best one yet.

I remember writing his card, knowing it might be his last birthday. I poured my heart into that card, explaining how much he meant to me and how lucky I was to have a dad like him—a dad who showed up, a dad who built me up yet didn't let me wallow if I felt sorry for myself. He had changed my life. I wanted to succeed so he'd be proud of me. He was my biggest cheerleader, confidant, and the person I went to when I was down. And there was nothing like an Ed Duffy hug. I can still feel it to this day. He always smelled like a mixture of Old Spice and mint. He was warm and loving and always had the best advice.

I remember confiding in my boss, Aileen, at the time. I told her the prognosis and shared I was not going to be okay when/if he passed away. And while this seems normal, it was hard for me to share because I knew I would cry. I thought crying in front of my boss must be some sort of mark that would diminish my potential. But Aileen leaned in, with great empathy, and told me we would get through it. She said the business was there to support me, and she would help me through it. She reassured me I could take the time I needed with my family. In that moment of vulnerability, a trust was built that was much stronger than before. It was just what I needed to hear. It was so kind and caring, and I will never forget it or her.

Ed died on December 7, 2010. My mom called us over that morning. My three brothers, my mother, and I stood around him. I held his hand; it was fragile and weak. I don't believe he was very conscious. All I remember is telling him it was okay to go, that we all loved him and would always keep him with us. I kissed his forehead, and he was already a little cool. He took his last breath with his family all around him. The oxygen left the room. All life stopped for that moment. My brothers were crying buckets of tears, my mom left the room, and I stood there and held his hand, trying to take him in—the man who made me believe in myself and taught me what a loving male figure should be. My brother Scott told me I was so strong because I wasn't crying. I wasn't crying because my brain didn't want to accept that this was the outcome. I couldn't, or I would crumble.

When we looked outside that morning, a huge rainbow was in the sky, seemingly based in our backyard. It was an amazing sight. I still choose to believe that God was happily welcoming in this Irish man and reminding us that life still held a pot of gold.

I tried to hold it together for the next year, mostly because my mom was so torn apart, and I felt like I had to be strong for her. I couldn't cry for a long time. I closed myself off and did everything possible to avoid feeling anything. It was a challenging year. I unraveled during this time and felt disconnected from everyone, especially Jack. My mom started to recover a bit in November 2011. Almost like clockwork, I fell apart. As if I finally had permission to let go, and then it swallowed me up emotionally.

My saving grace during this time was that heart-centered leadership from Aileen. She saw the impact the situation had on me and, instead of pushing me away or feeling like it was an area to avoid, she leaned in and asked me what I needed. She supported my working with my executive coach to get through this dark period, and that experience helped set me free. By sharing what was going on in my life and learning to invite someone in, I opened myself up to experience the care, empathy, and support I needed to receive help and find freedom.

ASK FOR HELP

Prior to the work I did on accessing my vulnerability, I would sooner jump off a bridge than ask for help. I viewed asking for help as a sign of weakness and failure. I loved giving help but did not want to admit I couldn't do something. The irony here is that most people who won't accept help genuinely love helping people. They just don't give themselves enough grace to accept it.

RELATIONSHIP MATRIX EXERCISE

People often ask my advice on knowing who to build relationships with within the workplace. I advise them to make a spreadsheet with the following columns: Advocates/Sponsors, Mentors, and Blockers. Advocates and Sponsors are people who can help your career. They may be in a role you want, see something special in you, or express an interest in your career. They aren't your boss but could clear ways for your career. Mentors have a skill or knowledge you can learn from. Blockers are people who seem to be a thorn in your side. They tweak or annoy you yet are in roles that could impede your progress. These people are important to know as well. We usually learn the most from people who annoy us, and if they can block your career, you need a plan to break that barrier.

Once you have those names, fill in the columns and think through a cadence to reach out to them. I generally advise quarterly check-ins as a start, in whatever medium works for the person. It could be email, a Zoom meeting, a coffee outside of work, a formal mentoring arrangement, volunteering for a project important to them, etc. You architect this part. Being intentional and transparent in your ask is very important. As I have said more than once, most people like to be seen as experts. They want to be wanted for their knowledge. Don't shy away from asking someone for a conversation to get the ball rolling.

Our willingness to ask for help is rooted in how we view ourselves. Are we worthy of help? Our worthiness stems from the foundational relationships around us and is, thus, worth exploring.

Being afraid to ask for help is one of the biggest mistakes I see people make in the workplace. I had to learn that asking for help was not a sign of weakness; it was a sign of strength. Have the courage to reach out and let people in. When you are at the beginning of your career or starting a new role, the help you ask for will determine your trajectory of success. The benefits of asking for help far outweigh the risks. Let me show you:

BENEFITS	RISKS
Most people love feeling like experts. Your asking for help validates them.	People might question your competence or abilities.
You develop closer relationships within your team as you bond over tasks and projects.	They might say no.
You help build a culture where asking for help is normalized and encouraged.	No risk
You get to learn the strengths of your team members and the spaces and tasks they thrive in.	No risk
And most importantly: you get the help you need.	Huge benefit!

When you ask for help, you invite someone to share that issue with you. The vulnerability creates a bond, and it brings much-needed support. Don't suffer in silence. Ask for help. Give people the gift you are so willing to give.

**

Vulnerability can be messy and hard and nuanced. Still, when we utilize the principles of heart-centered leadership—when we engage with curiosity, compassion, and approachability—we create a space where we can connect with others through past life events or current struggles.

I used to think that if I was positive, fun, and goal-oriented, people would just see my connection with them. But I've realized that it's most important for leaders to be vulnerable and caring. Vulnerability is really scary, but what scares me even more is thinking about the relationships and moments I would have missed out on in life had I not chosen to be vulnerable in key moments.

VULNERABILITY

Steel Backbone:
Choosing to be vulnerable is incredibly courageous. Whenever someone lets you in or is vulnerable with you, highlight the strength it took for them to be open. When we create an environment of trust and support, our team gets stronger. Remember, vulnerability takes practice. Start small and build that muscle.

How can you check in with your team regularly? What are you doing to create an environment of vulnerability?

Soft Heart:
Being vulnerable with your team about your story helps break down some walls that might hinder people from seeing the humanity of their leaders and asking for help when they need it.

Share your story with others, vulnerably. We are not meant to be perfect. Start small and share your fears and dreams. You will find this makes you more approachable, and the result for you is freedom.

CHAPTER 7

SELF-ASSURANCE

Examine Where You Get Your Strength

Self-assurance. It is a powerful word. For so long, I centered my career around a close sister of this word: confidence. Confidence is funny because you can appear outwardly confident yet be inwardly insecure. Self-assurance is similar to confidence yet has a meaningful nuance. Self-assurance means that at your core, you have faith in your strengths. You know that you are able—able to take risks, able to meet new challenges, able to stake claims, and, most important, able to deliver. Self-assurance means you can assure yourself of your ability. Sometimes, people can manufacture or fake their confidence. I did this for years as I hid many fears. Self-assurance requires honesty with yourself and authenticity.

The key to self-assurance is to detach yourself from outcomes, failures, and the judgment of others. You can do this by getting very clear on what makes you special and being grateful for all aspects of yourself. When you detach your self-worth from the outcomes, you start to depersonalize the things around you. This action bolsters your belief in yourself and reinforces that others' behaviors don't define you.

One of the biggest mistakes I see leaders make is deriving their self-worth from the validation of others. If we give someone that power, we provide them with the ability to take it away. When this happens, we need to come back to our origin story and figure out when we first began practicing this behavior. We must track the behavior up to the current moment to change the narrative in our minds. We need to own our power and not get entangled in the behaviors and judgments of others. Rewriting this limiting belief is how we start.

DETACH YOURSELF FROM OUTCOMES

I used to fight hard for the outcomes I wanted. I have since learned this is a counterproductive approach, because I would feel small if I didn't win or get the desired outcome. It created a barrier with people because I felt that they did not share my vision or drive. I wanted control. Like most things in my life, I learned this leadership lesson through a personal story.

I tried to find my birth mother, Barbara, after I had Marlie. I was thirty at the time. I wanted to know if we had any medical history in the family that I should know about. My mom, Jan, was 100 percent on board, and she called the doctor she had worked with on my adoption, Dr. Crozier. A funny thing happened— Dr. Crozier pretended to have no recollection of the experience. Nothing. We asked about his daughter. He claimed she had no recollection either. He has passed away now, so we can't dig deeper, but I can only surmise he had made a promise to the Biancos, and we were getting too close. It was such a disappointment, and it seemed so unfair. I felt cheated and angry. I was so close and could not believe he would not comply. This experience contributed to me feeling ashamed of my story, and I let go of finding my biological mother with a strong sense of unhappiness. I retreated and let the experience reinforce my feelings of unworthiness.

Then in 2020, I had a breakthrough. Through ancestry.com, I found a first cousin. I had to look at the match on the website several times to believe it. I contacted her, and she was vested in figuring out our relationship. I shared the adoption story and, sure enough, she confirmed her uncle had been part of a relationship as a teen where they gave the baby away. I couldn't believe my luck. I had spent years chasing a father figure, and suddenly here one was. So, she spoke to her dad, who agreed to speak to his brother. I absolutely could not believe what was happening. And I was terrified because rejection was still a possibility.

And like many things, the thing I had feared the most did, in fact, happen. He did not wish to revisit this time in his life and said he didn't want to be in contact. I felt the pain of that rejection, but you know what? It didn't break me, change my view of me, or send me down a shame spiral. This time, I just accepted that my biological father was on his own journey, and if that included not knowing his only biological child, then that was his decision to make. It didn't make me any less than. I now know his name is Herb and that has given me a name and an end point to this lifelong question of where I came from. I found peace within myself.

To my biological mother and father, I thank you for my life. Your purpose was to give me away to have this fantastic journey. And with that, I was able to rewrite my story and focus on the many gifts I have to offer. I have learned from you that you don't always get to choose the outcome in life, but you can do your part to make the best of it.

Detaching yourself from an outcome will always lead to more happiness and joy. Sometimes closure comes in different forms. Open yourself up to that and accept that you can't change people, but you can change your viewpoint and the type of impact you let them have on you.

FACE FAILURE

We all get married, thinking it will last forever. I was married to Jack for twenty years. In those years, Jack and I had three amazing daughters, amassed a decent amount of wealth, and made wonderful friends and memories. I will never regret those years. But in the span of two decades, I changed and evolved, and suddenly what once was life-sustaining became life-straining. It was not an outcome I expected.

We slowly grew apart. The saying goes that the first cut is the deepest, and for me, it was the disconnect over our miscarriages. I needed more support, and we didn't address it. When bigger issues came, we were already standing on a shaky foundation.

The second cut for me is what I call a festering wound. This wound stemmed from my sudden acceleration at work at Mars that created a subconscious power struggle. Suddenly my pay increased greatly, and the wage gap between Jack and me was large. I didn't see the issues at first, and neither did he. We were both excited to have more money. We enjoyed the spoils it afforded. Like many women who start to advance in their careers, we had to have the difficult and necessary discussion on whose job would take precedence. Jack didn't want to be diminished, and even though I would never purposely make him feel that way, he felt he had to take a strong stand to remain equal. We never really could agree on whose role would take precedence because Jack always stated his job was as important as mine. And with three young kids and both vying to have the "lead" career, we walked into a lot of landmines.

I underestimated the importance of being very direct and clear on the career discussion. My lack of clarity created issues that got bigger with time, and we subconsciously took on different roles that only pulled us further apart. If you are at a similar crossroads, be clear and sit in the discomfort of this discussion. If you sweep the hard things under the rug, they come back bigger than the first issue.

A big part of the breakdown of our marriage was a million little things left unaddressed. What we mistook for taking the high road or not sweating the small stuff was actually us avoiding uncomfortable issues. We just didn't like to open up or be uncomfortable in our emotions. Our foundation was shaky because we had both been hurt, but we would never rock the boat to confront those issues. We glossed over all the fissures in our foundation. This created problems when things really got heavy.

Years went by, and there were hurts on both sides—big hurts. And we just kept smiling and moving forward. And you know the saying: hurt people hurt people. When I started to pull away, I then had to justify it in my mind and, for a while, I made Jack into a bad person. And that couldn't be further from the truth. He is a very good person and a great dad. We were just unhealthy together.

The more I advanced in my career, the more I felt he wanted to make me small. And the smaller I felt, the more I wanted to lash out and have adventures that didn't include him. I really hurt him during this period because I would ignore many of his attempts to connect. I was growing and becoming stronger, and he didn't want to grow with me. We were both at fault.

We spent about seven years on a seesaw of ups and downs. Do we stay in it or not? The decision to get divorced was a very difficult one for someone like me. Someone who feared no one would ever love her. Someone who felt stronger and safer with someone to hold her hand. I needed someone there to ensure I was safe. It was primal for me. I didn't want to fail at marriage, I wanted my kids to have a solid foundation, and I desperately feared what others might think.

Tying our identity to our success or failure does not lend itself to self-compassion. If we aren't taking care of ourselves or our needs because we are afraid of the outcome or what other people might think, then we are not leading with a steel backbone. Sometimes we fail. That's just the truth of it. But we can choose to wallow in it, or we can choose to keep our chin up and backbone straight because we know that failure does not ultimately define us.

DISENGAGE FROM JUDGMENT

Divorce, in general, is not for the faint of heart. It is the hardest decision you will ever make, especially if kids are involved. And in this challenging, gut-wrenching time, people start to get involved with their opinions. It is like a game of telephone where everyone is trying to figure out who was at fault, and the story gets more salacious. I had made a conscious decision not to go into details about our personal life. And in this vacuum, the speculation churned. And I suddenly lost many friends, friends who had previously commiserated with me over the struggles of marriage. And some of these women whom I thought were my friends had no problem gossiping about me and blaming me for being a working woman, among other things.

During this time, three camps of my "friends" emerged: (1) those who loved the salacious part of this, wanted to gossip, and find a villain, (2) those who felt threatened because I was a working woman who left her man, and (3) those who decided just to be my friend (and thank God for each of you!). If you do the math, it means I lost a lot of my friends. And many were the parents of our daughters' friends, so it felt even more awful as it impacted the girls. One so-called "close friend" decided it would be fun to establish teams and went on a campaign that all moms should be "Team Jack." The truth here is that this whole division of teams hurt my children a lot more than it hurt me. Divorce is hard for everyone. Don't add to it by piling on hurtful gossip.

If one of your friends is going through a divorce, try to be "Team Family" and not get caught up in its drama. Instead, try to be empathetic to both sides. The kids don't benefit from others trying to take sides. You never know what happens behind closed doors, so please resist the urge to be judge and jury if this happens to someone you know.

Jack and I are now almost four years passed our divorce. It could have been easy to get mired in a failed outcome and judgment. It was not easy for any of us, but we celebrate special occasions and holidays together, people have calmed down on choosing sides, and our kids are very well adjusted. We were never good at communication but are finding our way. We both want our kids to have a great relationship with each other, which helps in the tougher moments. It was hard to revisit some of our hurts in this book, and I want to clarify that I also had fault in our divorce. I present these stories here to illustrate how I felt through it, but I had failings on my side too. Jack is a great person, and whoever he ends up with will receive a very kind soul.

People want to attach judgment, shame, and failure to divorce. While marriage shouldn't be viewed as disposable, sometimes it doesn't work out. That doesn't mean either person is bad. Let people divorce with dignity and respect. And unless you are the husband or wife, keep your opinions to yourself. When you separate the person from the outcome, it is a lot easier to embrace the humanity of all involved. When I learned to detach my views of myself from this outcome, I could move forward confidently.

This is also true for staying in careers that don't serve us. We can be afraid to make a change. We can tie our identity to our work, making us stay too long. Stay close to who you are, what you need in life, and don't let fear keep you in something you've outgrown. Sure, change can be daunting, but the other side will always be worth it if you jump in wholeheartedly and with purpose.

People will always have opinions about the way you do things. As people, we often judge those who do things differently than we do. You can't change that fact, but you can change the way you respond to judgments and criticism. Don't let the fear of judgment stop you from pursuing your best life, and don't let the reality of judgment shrink your potential or momentum. You were made for big things. Of course, people will talk about it; but don't let them stop you.

FIND WHAT MAKES YOU COME ALIVE

It's important to talk about where we shouldn't derive our self-assurance—we should not look to people or outcomes. So, where do we divert our attention? I think if more of us focused on what makes us come alive, what fills us with purpose and joy, then we would have much more stability in the department of self-assurance.

Nothing trained me more for the role of being a self-assured, purposeful businesswoman than my time in athletics. According to a global Ernst & Young survey, 94 percent of women who hold a C-Suite position are former athletes.[10] What's more, 52 percent played sports at the collegiate level.[11] There is an actual correlation between athleticism and business success—the discipline, the focus, the failures, the resilience, and the strength. The most successful people I know learn to fail and learn from it. They learn to work harder and push forward even when it feels really hard and uncomfortable. Sports taught me how to win and, more important, how to lose gracefully. No one hates losing more than me, but I've learned to pause and try to find a purpose in it.

I was a kid who lived entirely in my head, and playing sports helped me turn off my brain and focus on the task at hand. It enabled me to be fully present in the moment. And because I was "chosen" for the team, I felt included. Being chosen has always followed me in all aspects of my life.

I played basketball from age ten to eighteen. I played in high school through the end of my junior year, and I always started as point guard because I was fast. I was known for playing great defense because I was tenacious; I wanted that ball. At 5'2", this was a feat. This experience taught me that no matter what your perceived weaknesses are, if you want the ball badly enough, if you want the leadership position, the promotion, the raise badly enough, you have to release any limiting beliefs from within or around you. You need to fight for it, get in the game, and surprise a few people with your talent.

I realized fairly young that you have to be willing to dream big. When I started playing sports, I had some odds stacked against me. Mainly my size—people often dismissed me because of it. I would walk onto most teams with the swagger that I was going to bring something great to the team. Sports taught me how to carry myself confidently, although it took a lot of time to learn. I carried this thinking into the work world. Confidence isn't always within, and often you do just have to jump in, work on your skills, and find the love in whatever you are doing. There is value in achievement, and hard work translates into peak performance even if you are missing some key skills. Your attitude determines your outcome, always.

I started playing softball from the time I was ten to throughout college. It became my biggest passion and helped me come alive. I remember being at Nationals for softball during the 1984 Olympics. It was the year of Mary Lou Retton and the Women's Gymnastics team. I remember thinking, *I want to be as great at my sport as she is at hers.* And it bolstered me that she was tiny too. Tiny but powerful. And expressive in succeeding. She was not about being seen and not heard. It was okay in the Olympics for women to win and to celebrate. I loved this, and it made me feel okay to have a swagger in my step, a swagger that said, *I know I'm good, and I'm okay with that.* I realized that it's advantageous to know your worth and talent and not be shy about owning that. Own your talent. It's okay to be quietly confident, but never diminish yourself or play small to make others feel better.

What we're drawn to at a young age influences our passion and purpose as adults. Sports may not be what motivated you or people in your life. But there is always something. Find your passion; find what makes you feel truly alive and truly free. And if you are a parent, let your kids try different things and then see what *they* like, what gives them that fiery "I'm on top of the world" sparkle in their eye. That's where you find the magic. Learning how to play big and feeling confident about your role in whatever you do is truly freeing.

Finding your purpose and passion doesn't mean you need a job that aligns perfectly with those passions. I never went pro with sports or coached softball. Instead, I found elements of jobs that I was passionate about. Excelling in your career is less about the role and more about your ability to find aspects of the role that give you a sense of purpose and align with what you are passionate about. I see this every day in my current job at SmileDirectClub. People in all areas of the business are aligned with the purpose of making people smile and bringing joy to people's lives. Many people are not in their destination role yet. They are working toward it. However, this North Star, this uniting purpose of transforming lives, transcends individual roles and enables everyone to feel connected to a greater good. I see people work through minor annoyances each day because they feel connected to purpose. Make sure you know your purpose and work for someone who enables you to express your passion.

When you find what makes you come alive and what fills you with a sense of purpose, chase it. Don't chase it for the outcome or the people involved; chase it for that feeling of wholeness and warmth. That's genuine self-assurance.

***

When we are self-assured of our own identity, strengths, and purpose, we can face less-than-ideal outcomes, failures, and others' judgments with grace and self-respect. Those things will still knock us down from time to time, but when we are self-assured of our steel backbones and soft hearts, we can walk into any situation knowing it will not defeat us.

HEART-CENTERED LEADERSHIP LESSON
SELF-ASSURANCE

Steel Backbone:

You are going to face failure. If you don't, you are not living. Accepting that failure is part of life is critical. Joseph Campbell said, "Where you stumble, there lies your treasure."[12] You can dismiss regret if you instead choose to learn from experiences of failure.

Think about times you have failed. What did you make it mean? How did it change you? How can you release yourself from judgment? How can you detach yourself from an outcome?

Soft Heart:

We make a true transformation when we shift our energy from "doing" to "being." There is a delivery and execution that is required for all jobs. The shift here is doing something for validation versus just being yourself and believing you are worthy just for who you are.

When you are working today, remind yourself of your inherent worthiness.

CHAPTER 8

COURAGE

Turn Adversity into Triumph

Someone once asked me how I'd describe beauty. When I thought about it, I realized that, for me, beauty is always about courage. There's nothing as striking or inspiring as someone who steps forward, tackles a challenge, and bravely faces a tough moment.

Courageous people grow throughout their lives. They embrace new information, learn continuously, and work authentically with the people around them, building relationships and trust.

Courage is at the core of heart-centered leadership. In fact, the root of the word "courage", *couer* in French, means heart. Courage is required to be authentic, compassionate, and caring. We need courage to invite emotions into the leadership space.

I like to tell my daughters that risk is part of life. There are no mistakes, just lessons learned. They've heard me say it a million times—probably so much that they're tired of it! But I hope they grow up seeing bravery as an exciting, beautiful trait.

When I'm coaching new leaders, I try to help them see the

beauty of courage too. Of course, there are the big, audacious moments when an individual or team takes a monumental leap, and everyone can see and applaud the impact. But there are everyday moments that deserve recognition too—whether it's a shy person speaking up for the first time or a new manager admitting a mistake. Great leaders encourage and celebrate these moments. They're also there as support afterward, when the person might be thinking, *Did I say too much?* or *Did I do the wrong thing?* I know those thoughts enter my head after I try something new. These are important times for validation. A manager can help turn courage into a career-enhancing habit by offering support and reinforcement.

Whether you are seizing a business opportunity, righting a wrong, being your authentic self with the people around you, or confronting a manager who doesn't listen to you, courage matters. And acting with courage gets easier the more you do it—it's a muscle you can stretch and grow.

COURAGE IN LEADERSHIP AND LIFE

I grew up thinking I could conquer anything and, with enough grit and determination, win at all I do: school, sports, you name it. I was largely blessed with good teachers, coaches, and bosses in my life. In some ways, I was naïve to what so many people go through— abusive or oppressive behavior from peers or authority figures. Then I had an experience at work that shook me to my core.

After years as an overachiever who always delivered on goals and won praise from my bosses and teams, I took a new assignment at my company and got a boss who couldn't see my value. Instead, he actively belittled and undermined me in front of my peers, my team, and the organization.

He set out on a mission to make my life a living hell from day one. He didn't want me in my role and sometimes passive-aggressively, sometimes aggressively, made sure his opinions were known to all, including me. And for the next eighteen months, I endured mistreatment and bullying at work.

He dismissed my experience, ignored my counsel, talked over me in meetings, and disparaged me to my peers and my team. Everyone saw it, but no one did anything about it. He threatened to fire me if I talked to anyone outside of our team because he was insecure about my relationship with others at the company. He pitted peers against me, believing "no one kills you quicker than your peers," which he used to say to me frequently. We once had a meeting to introduce a new HR Shared Services model, and he asked the guest speakers from corporate whose head would be on the block if it failed. The speakers were uncomfortable but ultimately admitted, "Cheryl is responsible in this unit," and he gleefully smiled. I knew he'd do everything possible to tank that project. And the dread and hopelessness I felt seeped into every part of my life.

His abuse was systemic and convincing. I could name at least ten more examples, from inciting my team of direct reports to reject me, to a performance review that concluded I was too "put together" to be liked, to whispering that my peers thought I was weak as I was about to introduce myself on my first day. Many colleagues saw me struggling yet did nothing about it. And I was HR, so there was no one to whom I could voice my complaints.

I lost every bit of confidence I had.

Don't let your people lose their humanity. Step in and help. It could be the difference between life and death. I became very lonely from the isolation I felt, and, at this time, I also was feeling the weight of my house mortgage. I lived in fear every day for eighteen months that I would be fired, which scared me to death. There were mornings I'd wake up with the thought of going to work and facing this guy, and I thought it might just be better if I just wasn't alive. I felt ashamed, and shame goes after your identity. He had broken me thoroughly and completely. I felt like my kids would be homeless and embarrassed of me. I didn't even think I could get another job anywhere, doing anything. To say it was debilitating is an understatement.

I had several courageous conversations with this boss. I called out our dysfunction and asked him to name his issues with me. He was not transparent. I continued to try my old methods to win him over by overachieving and proving my worth. I kept thinking, *If he sees what a star I am, he'll like me.* Well, he didn't. I tried to acquiesce to some of his demands, which made me feel worse about myself. I kept at it for eighteen months. It was the worst time in my life because it felt like it had no end. The athlete in me wouldn't let me quit even though this experience was slowly killing my joy, sense of self, and ability to live my life.

I can remember talking to Judy. She suggested I might be depressed. I couldn't have a conversation without crying, and I felt like I had no one to turn to. I was in a very dark place. I just couldn't find any positivity in life. My marriage was crumbling, and my work life was killing me. And then I hit rock bottom. When you hit rock bottom, you have two choices: stay there and die within or start to climb out slowly. It was the breaking point that could have led to a breakdown. But with the help and support of people who believed in me and constantly reminded me who I was, I found a way out.

We had a breakthrough when he got a new boss. This boss was willing to call him out on his bad behavior, and he suddenly had some accountability. The combination of this and his realization that I wasn't going away started to change his view of me. We began to work together, and he finally said to me, "I like the way we are working." The sad thing is that we could have had this relationship the whole time. I threatened him because of my relationships with others. He couldn't see how I could use those relationships to help him. His ego wouldn't let him. It was the worst experience I've had as a woman in the workplace. But I did survive it. I stood in the fire, found my courage and sense of self, and fought my way out. When I left that team, I did so from a place of strength, which has been a magnifying effect on my sense of empowerment and self-assurance.

In retrospect, I held on for longer than I should have, but it was easier to think that holding on was better for my family. It was easy to diminish my needs and be afraid. I had done this my whole life. Never again. Sometimes we shut down because we feel we deserve what we are receiving. You don't deserve to be bullied. If you find yourself in this situation, get the right people around you to support you and help you determine the next steps. Sometimes the lies get so loud that you need people who speak the truth.

LOOKING BACK, LEARNING, AND GROWING

This decade of my life represented the breaking down of who I thought I was, who I was pretending to be. It sounds trite to say it was transformational, but it was a total and humbling rebirth that took extreme courage. I had spent my life building this image: mom, wife, successful worker, had it all together, impenetrable. I had handcrafted my safety raft. My ego was the leading force, and it had me on the wrong path. Thankfully, my coaching partners helped me deconstruct my ego, image, and armor around my heart. What remained was more authentic. I came out of that season with a stronger backbone and a softer heart.

I still carry some scars from these experiences. There are times when I feel real PTSD from the bullying. But as I regained confidence and fought through those experiences, I reclaimed myself and my life.

When the next opportunity came along, I was running toward something great, not running away from something bad. That perspective—that I was finally controlling my destiny from a place of wholeness—made all the difference in the world.

The opportunities that came out of these adversities were some of the most remarkable experiences of my life. I'm grateful for the heart-centered leaders who surrounded me during this time and encouraged me to be courageous even as I was walking through fire. As a leader, don't miss those situations where you can address the humanity of what someone is going through. Just some moments of kindness could save someone from destruction.

SMALL STEPS FORWARD

Courage in the workplace takes many different forms. Your act of courage may look different from your coworkers' acts of courage, and that's okay—it's even good. Courage is what enables you to overcome obstacles, take on giants, and turn adversity into triumph.

Maybe you have a coworker who is not on your side. Maybe you have an idea that would benefit your team but you're afraid to voice it. Maybe you want a promotion or a raise but second-guess your qualifications. Whatever situation you find yourself in, find ways to take steps forward. Celebrate small moments of courage— like showing up to work even when you feel crippling anxiety, or speaking up in a staff meeting to make your opinion known. When we take small steps forward and they don't defeat us, we gain the confidence to take those bigger steps.

Remember that courage comes from the heart. You don't have to shut down your feelings or humanity to face situations with courage—quite the opposite. When you detach yourself from outcomes and root your identity in your core values and inherent worthiness, you can step forward in courage with strength and heart, knowing that with each step of courage, you are walking toward your purpose.

HEART-CENTERED LEADERSHIP LESSON
COURAGE

Steel Backbone:
Life will throw obstacles at you. Use the resources and people around you. Please don't suffer in silence. Things may not go the way they say it does in books. Stay true to yourself, and don't judge yourself. Have courage and just honor your journey.

Are there areas in your life you are avoiding? How can you look at those areas with courage?

Soft Heart:
Adversity makes it easy to put on armor to avoid being seen and protect your heart. Armor will never serve you if you want to experience deep, intimate love with someone else. Or even a deep friendship. Have the courage to keep an open heart and the courage to let yourself shine.

CHAPTER 9

RESILIENCE

Learn from the Unexpected

"**R**esilience" is a word I know well. It has been part of what many leaders have said about me. And while I'm grateful for this attribute, it came from a lot of pain and loss. I believe that resilience is linked to a positive outlook in life and the perspective of trying to make the best of whatever life throws at you.

Did you know that hearts can be kept alive for up to twenty-four hours after death?[13] Hearts are resilient. When we live, lead, and love with our hearts at the center, we build resiliency that is unmatched in the world we live in today. Rather than centering our ventures, accomplishments, and interactions from a cold and strictly mind-centered place, we can approach our daily lives with a softness that will, in turn, strengthen us.

I talked previously about my work experience with bullying, and, honestly, that required all the resilience I could ever muster. I thought I would never experience something so shattering until grief hit me one more time.

RESILIENCE IN THE FACE OF GRIEF

Heading back into dating at forty-eight is a little bit like a death. A part of you dies—the married you, the comfortable you, the you who likes to wear comfy clothes. And a new part of you emerges. It seems fun at first. Getting back out there. Having an assortment of people at your fingertips, multiple dates, new experiences. That being said, I could write a separate book on all the weird experiences I had while online dating. I hated the whole artifice of it. Most people were not who they said they were, which was the opposite of what I stood for. It got so old, and the point of bringing it up here is to share that by November 2019, I had decided I just wanted to meet someone the old-fashioned way—locking eyes and being interested in knowing someone more. And then, magically, one month later, I met Matthew in a bar while celebrating my birthday with a friend.

It is like those sayings that when you least expect something, it happens. Matthew and I had a natural and easy connection. We made each other laugh hard, the kind of laugh where you end up crying, doubled over. Matthew could command a room, and I liked that. He had a natural way with people and was very chivalrous. We spent fifteen months together during COVID, getting closer along the way without the distraction of regular life and eventually falling in love. This relationship was fun and intense as we both realized the specialness of what we had found. Yet it had its struggles too.

He was in the grueling stages of a contentious divorce that was causing him a lot of pain. By February 2021, we were in discussions about marriage and the next steps after his divorce. We were hoping for resolution in March. I loved him, and he loved me. I provided a safe place for him to land and a renewed sense of purpose, which he would later give to me. I could go on for pages about the fun we had and the love we shared; however, it was a ride short-lived.

One week, we experienced a lot of built-up tension in our relationship. He had started drinking too much to deal with the pain of his divorce. Matthew was about to leave for a boys' trip with one of his friends, and I didn't want him to go. I had an eerie feeling that something bad was going to happen to him. In fact, on the Wednesday before he departed, I told him he needed to ensure that his brother or friends had my number, just in case. He felt my worry was unfounded, and I felt his stance on being invincible was problematic. So, I said goodbye to him, feeling very uncertain and a little pissed.

I realized on Friday that my anger wasn't serving him; my ego was trying to control him and the situation. I had an epiphany while getting a facial that I just wanted him to feel loved because I knew love was the path out of his pain. And I would be there for him as we dealt with the drinking issues. I texted him words that he so appreciated, although they were not the stuff of a Hallmark card. I said, "I fucking love you, Matthew Frye, and that's all that matters."

He responded, "This could be the best thing you've ever texted me."

That Saturday morning, he called me with such love in his voice. He was feeling good but said he wished he was back in Tennessee at my house. Sometimes we cut short some calls because we are busy. I am so glad that on that day, I just sat down and listened to him talk about his excitement about our future. I feel so fortunate for that sweet two-hour phone call because just a few hours later, in a nice restaurant, Matthew passed away suddenly and unexpectedly by choking on a piece of food. And even though his friend was a doctor, it wasn't enough to save his life.

I got the call on Sunday morning, on my way to Jessie's soccer game. His brother tracked me down. I knew something was off because Matthew usually texted me frequently, and I hadn't heard from him since 5:00 p.m. the previous night. That was highly irregular. The memory of that call is so painful. His brother had me pull over, and at that point, I just thought he had hurt himself skiing. And then the words came through the phone—he had passed away. I went into shock at that moment. I started driving again and called Judy. I remember she made me breathe because I was on the verge of hyperventilating. She stabilized me; thank God for her. I proceeded to the soccer game because I didn't want to disappoint Jessie, and I couldn't think straight. I found one of my friends, a fellow soccer mom who knew Matthew and me, and told her what happened somewhat vacantly. She had me sit down. I just couldn't fathom that Matthew was gone. I sat and tried to grasp this shocking information.

The next week was a blur. I couldn't stop shaking and wasn't eating much. My mother and friends rallied around me, and I'm so grateful for them. Grief is a funny thing. It weaves a strange and different course. I had lived through the death of Ed, which was shattering, and this was a totally different feeling. I thought Matthew would be my happily-ever-after, and now he was gone in such an unexpected way. It was hard to accept. His life was cut short at forty-eight, with children who still needed him. I just kept waiting for the punchline of this callous joke. It was hard to make it through the days without crying for the loss of his life, our future, and the sheer cruelty of losing someone this way.

There were a lot of complexities around his divorce and in his passing. But like all things in this book, what's important is the meaning I made of our relationship and his untimely death. I spent the next few weeks trying to understand why God would give me this person just to take him away. Why did I have to suffer in silence? And why, when Matthew was so close to having what he wanted, did he have that chance ripped away? I was distraught and became obsessed with near-death stories because I had to know where he was. My intellectual mind had an idea, but my heart needed certainty. It comforted me to hear the stories of those who had "crossed over," and I started to believe he was indeed in a better place. I went through all the stages of grief and found myself equally angry and sad on most days. My experience with coaching guided me to find a glimmer of hope in all of this. I went to grief counseling, which I highly recommend to anyone who has lost someone. I poured out all I felt, and my mood slowly began to shift.

Here is where the resilience of my past came into being in a helpful way. I knew to ask for help and seek counseling, I made sure to prioritize self-care, I relied on my advocates, and I frequently reminded myself of my purpose.

I was determined to ensure that Matthew's life had not been in vain and that his purpose in my life was to deliver me to something bigger. The only way I could make peace with his passing was to give it purpose. In that discovery, I jotted down a few key goals:

1. I will never settle for a smaller love again.
2. I will be there for my kids in the moments that matter.
3. I will live the biggest life possible and not settle.
4. I will keep my heart open and expand it to love even deeper.
5. I will finally write the book I know I have in me.
6. I will start a business once I finish with the corporate world.
7. I will expand my faith.

And this process of building resilience freed me to find a new purpose. I have a different view of grief now. People talk a lot about the five stages of grief, but I know there should be a sixth one, as purpose provided me with the most healing. In this place, I could see how God had called Matthew home and that he was at peace. Matthew had come into my life to complete his journey—a journey to unconditional love. And in this renewed relationship with God, I was able to find peace for myself. I learned so much through my relationship with Matthew, and for that, I am forever grateful.

With Matthew, I could finally be myself and relax in a relationship as my full self. With him, I felt 100 percent lovable. He calmed the noise in my head as everything fell away. I learned what falling in love meant. I just don't think I was mature enough when I met Jack to get it and let it happen. Falling in love requires intimacy and trust that I didn't have to give previously, and I needed the self-assurance not to get enmeshed. Now that I have known the wonder and exhilaration, I know I have to experience this feeling again.

I found my voice with Matthew. I used to stay silent in relationships so as not to rock the boat. Our relationship was just not like this. We both voiced our opinions emphatically. I began to trust that you can be angry and disagree and not be left. Again, that old abandonment story began to recede in my mind. Its clutches no longer had the stranglehold from years past. And I emerged a softer, more loving person. I was no longer anchored in fear of losing those who love me the most. I no longer held back because of how devastating it would be to give my all and lose. And yet I did give my all, and I did lose, but I also gained so much. I gained confidence in my lovability and sense of self. I finally took my place as the nurturing female. I no longer needed anyone's approval. This relationship set me free. I learned to trust myself. And while I hate every moment of knowing that Matthew is gone, he changed everything for me, and that has made me a more vibrant, giving person who is finally ready for mutual, unbridled love.

It's funny, sometimes death can make you want to be absent from the world. Matthew's death made me want to embrace this one beautiful life more fully. Life has become more precious—a word he loved to use. He helped me overcome my proclivity to fly under the radar and hide. He unearthed a being who wanted to love more deeply and fully than she ever imagined. In Ed's death, I felt I would not be okay. And I set forth to make that statement true. In the bullying incident, I felt the loss of myself and thought I was not going to be okay, yet I also started to fight for myself. In Matthew's death, I felt so much love and support that I knew I would be okay. Even more, I learned that this epic event would be an invitation to live an even bigger life, where I no longer lived as if I was dying. I had seen death up close. I had been to the bottom. Now there was only one way out, which was up. Now, I could live my life fully and not wait one second. And at that moment, without fear, pretense, limiting beliefs, or ego, I took my final step as a heart-centered leader.

Matthew always liked to end a story with a takeaway. So, here's my takeaway. You can't always predict when love will walk in the door but don't let circumstance keep you from welcoming it. Not every relationship goes smoothly, but if you stay rooted in love, authenticity, and mutual appreciation, you can weather any storm. Loss is part of life, and it can feel gut-wrenching. Hell, it *is* gut-wrenching. I'm not trying to shorten anyone's grief or underestimate its impact. I still have my days when sorrow takes over. However, if you can take time to find the gifts, embrace them, and hold onto them, you can emerge stronger and more resilient. Give the pain a purpose in life and leadership!

RESILIENCE IN THE FACE OF ADVENTURE

I've not always been at ease with love. From feeling unlovable to being insecure in sharing who I truly was to letting the fear of rejection get in the way of genuine connection, love has been my most challenging journey.

When Matthew died, I had no idea if love would walk back through my door. And this is when the saying "when God closes a door, He opens a window" became a reality in my life. And what a window he opened. Here's what happened.

Several months after Matthew died, a friend texted me to see how I was , without knowing the full extent of my current situation. We had met a few years before and lightly kept in touch. I was able to help him connect with some local businesses when his work brought him to Nashville. I waited a bit to call him back, because how do you put in a text that your boyfriend died recently? When I shared the news with him, he had news of his own. He was recently divorced and had admired how I handled mine. He was hoping just to talk through life post-divorce. Both of us were wounded and needed healing, but it felt good to connect with someone going through something significant and sad which required starting over.

Mike and I started talking and checking in on each other. It wasn't long before frequently became daily. And little by little, our conversations shifted from expressing our sadness and emotions to learning more about each other. As we started sharing our interests and details about growing up, we found we had so much in common—even favorite movies and songs. Each of us made the other laugh, which felt novel and refreshing given the sorrow. We talked for four hours one night, and had we not had to go to work the next day, we probably could have gone longer. With each phone call, it felt harder to hang up. I know that sounds like middle school, but we never fell short on things to talk about. Given we lived in two different cities (he was in Atlanta), we would talk on FaceTime, which I usually hated, as did he. But it helped our connection deepen. I felt like I had known this person for a very long time, and we just clicked. It was a healthy connection.

We both shared a hesitation about this becoming a relationship too soon. I was grieving, as was he, but the attraction was undeniable. It was all there: the mental, emotional, physical, and spiritual connection. There were a few days when I thought for sure Ed, Matthew, and God were sitting in heaven and hatched a plan to deliver me the perfect man because of all I had been through—like I had earned angel wings or something. It was such a wonderful surprise to have this very sweet, very handsome, brilliant, and caring man become a bigger part of my life.

I couldn't wait to get a text or to talk. His positivity filled me up with hope. And he didn't mind hearing me talk about Matthew and where I was in my grieving process. I returned his kindness by listening to his feelings and emotions following his divorce. We had both been married for over twenty years and the help and support we provided each other just accelerated the friendship to be something more. Some days I felt guilty, but Matthew had been gone for what felt like forever, even though it was only months. I did have to grapple with those feelings and realize love knows no timeline, nor does grief. Mike was instrumental in my healing, and I hope I am in his.

And now, as I write this, I can confirm we have found love again. Both of us, mutually. We started to make trips to see each other and found that spark that makes you feel like you can take on any challenge and win. I have fallen for him completely, and I love how I feel.

I know some of you may feel like this can't possibly be. How could love blossom so soon? But here's what I know. After losing

Matthew, part of my grief work made me realize that my heart is now two sizes bigger. Now I can love more fully and freely. I feel more capable of loving and clearer on what I want. Mike was open and available. I believe he too wanted to live a big life full of love and affection. Our values aligned and danced happily together. Instead of connecting in the wound, we connected through love. The vulnerability stemming from our recent experiences created the opening to let in love. And everything with us just works.

Mike runs a cabling business and enjoys a great deal of success. He is smart and savvy and helps me think through my business challenges. He is a true partner who loves my business side, appreciates the athlete side of me, and makes me feel loved and appreciated for all the things that make me me. I shake my head sometimes because we met so late in life, but I know we will make the next fifty years an amazing journey. He is my great love, a love that feels deeper and purer than any other. I could have only found him by going through everything I did with Jack and Matthew. They enriched my life and opened me up in their own ways. What I learned from them enabled me to finally see and find my perfect match. Our lives are in separate cities, yet somehow we will cross this divide because love this big can't be limited by distance.

How to embrace the adventures in life:

1. Allow yourself to dream big. Too often, we set our own limitations. To quote my coach Judy, "How big do you want to be?"

2. Welcome in play as a part of life. We often get too serious about ourselves and our lives. Remember the carefree innocence of your youth and find those moments when you feel your soul expanding.

3. See adventure as a gift. Sometimes we are afraid to step into something unknown. Flip that on its head, open yourself to the possibilities, and see it as a stepping stone to something greater.

4. Let life emerge. We try to orchestrate our life to feel safe and under the illusion of control. Live in the moment and let yourself be surprised about what God has in store for you.

5. Know that you are worthy, deserving, and capable of unconditional and big love. Many of us struggle with feelings of unworthiness. This mentality will waste your potential. Know that you are worthy and made perfectly just the way you are. To quote *Moulin Rouge*, "The greatest gift we'll ever learn is to love and be loved in return."[14] Let yourself be loved in return!

MY TIPS FOR BUILDING RESILIENCY

Whether through grief or adventure, pain or joy, valleys or mountaintops, building resilience will enable you to lead, live, and love with optimism and hope. Building resiliency takes time; it doesn't happen overnight but in the depths of every season you find yourself in. How do you build your resilience? I have a few tips:

1. **Take time to list people who are 100 percent in your corner.** This can serve as a good reminder when you feel down. These are the people who will have your back and always remind you that you are not alone. Write these names down and what these people mean to you.

2. **Create a reminder that can bring you peace.** Create a mental safe place, and through a physical mechanism, remind yourself of it. My version of a safe place is the beach, my happy place. I fully picture myself there—the sights and smells. A beautiful day with blue skies, waves crashing. I'm in a long, flowing white dress and feeling loved and appreciated. You need a clear vision of what your safe place looks like and how you feel. Then, in this moment of imagination, I take my thumbnail and press it in my index finger, and I tell myself that when I feel this sensation, I should return to this place of total relaxation and support. I practiced this a bit, so whenever I feel my nerves or fear start to take over my emotions, I put that thumbnail into my index finger, and I immediately go back to this memory. The actual sensation of my nail into my finger pad sends a tactical feeling that takes my mind off my fear and to a place where I feel safe and secure.

3. **Find a physical outlet to release stress.** I will never forget when I had a physical and my doctor told me I imported a great deal of stress but didn't have an outlet to let it out of my body. She told me that this would turn into deeper stress or health issues over time. Make sure you export the stress that lives in your body. Your body will keep score here. I love to do yoga and walk with my dogs.

4. **Find the positive outcome through self-reflection.** I like to give my stress a purpose. Why is it here? What is it meant to teach me? Am I living my principles or stuck living someone else's? How can I reframe this stress into something empowering?

5. **Ask for help.** Getting the pain out of your body by talking about it will take power out of the pain. A shared experience becomes a shared support system.

6. **Practice self-care.** Eat well, drink water, and sleep. I know it sounds trite, but it does help settle your cerebral cortex, which gets hijacked when you are spiraling.

As you work toward heart-centered leadership, your resilience will naturally grow. Our hearts are solid and resilient things—and I think we all need to realize that more.

RESILIENCE

Steel Backbone:
Resilience helps us take on and process the unexpected with hope and purpose. Being a heart-centered leader requires resiliency because you need to adapt and learn from all of the unexpected things that happen on your team and in your life.

How can you bolster your resilience? What things make you spiral? What plans can you pre-think to help you through those moments?

Soft Heart:
Resilience is built over time throughout all different seasons in your life. You do not need to be going through a hard time to build resilience. You can build it by choosing adventure and commitment in your daily decisions.

What is one action you can take toward building resilience today?

CHAPTER 10

AUTHENTICITY

Choose Yourself and Own Your Story

As we come to the end of this book, and hopefully the beginning of a whole new chapter in your life, I want to encourage you to think back to your origin story and own all of it. When we own our stories and don't hide any part of ourselves from ourselves or others, we are truly living authentically. To experience the wholeness we all crave, we have to stop compartmentalizing our lives into different segments and, instead, bring the fullness of ourselves to every situation and aspect of our lives. Our life story is our leadership story.

I hope that the principles listed in this book, as well as the practices for incorporating those principles, will help you live more authentically than you ever thought possible. The world needs all of who you are—not just parts.

Just as we began by looking at our origin stories, I want us to reflect on our leadership stories as we close. Your leadership story is not just the titles written on your résumé. It explores the traits you've grown in, what you've accomplished, and how the way you lead impacts your life and vice versa.

I feel I've lived a few different lives so far: the abandoned child, the successful athlete, the wife and mother, the corporate executive, the survivor of loss, and a champion of heart-centered leadership.

Earlier in my career, I studied those above me and tried to adopt their traits as if they had the secret sauce for success. I morphed and changed and tried to match the energy and styles of those I reported to. I diligently studied leaders I respected and tried to be like them. Some of this was positive; some of it served as a way to hide my true nature.

I remember my shock after I started my coaching journey and spent more time in Human Resources. My Myers Briggs assessment shifted from an ENTP to an ENFP. I was previously categorized as Extroverted, Intuitive, Thinking, and Perceptive. I transformed the T to an F, which is Feeling.

In the past, I had worn the ENTP designation like a badge of honor. It was the most common style of leader at Mars, and I figured it meant I belonged. I had equated "Thinking" with strong leadership and "Feeling" with soft leadership. Yet once I took the time and space to know myself, I realized I had been hiding a very big heart in favor of appearing more logical and being seen as a critical thinker. Those traits seemed to be the success model of those I felt had "made it." Yet once I started to unzip my heart and let it show, it was hard to zip it back up. There is nothing wrong with a Thinking dimension, in fact it is a great trait! I just wasn't being true to myself and that was the big insight.

I spent years trying to hide my emotional side, and people could feel that—at work and in relationships. I feared that if I let my vulnerability show, I would not be safe, and I wouldn't survive. Vulnerability was like my kryptonite. But I had such a wrong view of it. And many of us do this. We hold at bay the one thing that can actually cure us. And it enables us to take the easy way out by avoiding the discomfort that necessitates any real breakthroughs.

Toward the beginning of my career, I didn't have the courage to stand firmly and with conviction. I was a chameleon who had learned to read a room and was so observant because I felt my life depended on the swaying emotions of those who controlled the decisions. Don't get me wrong, I would fight for what I wanted, but if someone disagreed or pushed back or was more senior than me, I would often give up too easily. I spent a lifetime trying to control every situation, even though control would not fully serve me. But I've learned that the only real choice we have is how we respond to any situation. Things will happen that we don't prepare for: people leave you, people die, you have a bad work situation. But the power is how we respond and what we make it mean.

As a woman, I had to learn a hard lesson on not giving my power away, both at work and in relationships. I used to put myself last, not share my true feelings, and endlessly try to please people. People-pleasing is exhausting, never-ending, and makes you play very small. It will never serve you. Now that I own my power, I'm no longer a chameleon and very comfortable having my voice heard.

It didn't come easy; it took work, focus, and intention. You can start owning your power by knowing your story, winning formula, values, limiting beliefs, and purpose. Own who you are, and don't change for anyone. Yes, you need to know your audience, but be unabashedly you, every day.

After years of breaking down my hard shell, I now happily embrace the F in my Meyers Briggs assessment. My big heart has helped me lead the way to more compassionate, inclusive, and diverse work environments where the humanity of each team member is acknowledged and prioritized. Becoming a heart-centered leader and being led by heart-centered leaders has given me the strength I didn't know I was capable of. It has increased my capacity to love myself and others in innumerable ways. It's a title I wear proudly.

FINDING MEANING THROUGH IT ALL

We are all works in progress. We think everyone else has it together, but we all have our pain. Some are just better at masking it. You have to learn to look back on what you've come through and genuinely appreciate the lessons and why life served them to you. As we strive to find the best version of ourselves, the important thing is to do the work and trust that our struggles are the things that make us human. Open the wounds, find your pain, and make it mean something positive. And as we get to the end here, I want to tie up a few loose ends and share some gratitude.

When I got the opportunity to join SmileDirectClub, I was ecstatic because the company's mission spoke directly to me: a company that wanted to make people smile. When the role became clear to me, I just knew this was a way to take the lessons from Ed forward. I mean, he asked me who I made smile every day when I came home from school. Now I would get to make millions of people smile. Ed's legacy lives on, and I get to honor him every day. It is one of the ways I keep him alive. I have brought my vulnerable, empathetic self to my company, and they are letting me instill heart-centered leadership as the core of our leadership curriculum. I know my dad proudly smiles down on me from his safe space in heaven.

My daughter, Marlie, came to intern in the summer of 2018. She pointed out that I'm often the only woman in the room or one of the few women. It struck me when she said that. She asked me how that felt. I took some time to reflect. I'm a woman who grew up with brothers (Eric, Gordon, Todd, and Scott) and played sports, which was a more male-oriented activity. I was born with a competitive drive to survive and a fight to prove my worth, which equipped me to play in a man's world. I still have my struggles, but I have embraced the power I bring, regardless of my gender.

I'm a survivor, I played sports at a higher level than most of my colleagues, and I've been to the bottom and fought my way back. I've always loved being a disrupter, and I love winning. I'm a competitor through and through: steel backbone, soft heart. And maybe that makes me a bit more like my counterparts. But here's the deal. Your style can't be winning at all costs because you will lose. You can't be cold and indifferent and think people will follow your lead. The old-school style of driving hard for numbers only and treating people like a commodity does not work. People want to work for people who have a purpose, create purpose-driven businesses, and have heart and passion for what they do and who they hire. You must focus on the humanity of those around you. And after COVID, we need empathy like we never have before.

My personality and my quest for heart-centered leadership don't always land with people wired to be harder and more driven. Every day, I meet people who only care about numbers and think vulnerability is a weakness. I accept that not all people understand why purpose, heart, authentic connection, and caring for your people matter. Some people still view me as soft. However, this perception is wrong. And your team engagement and productivity will falter if you turn away from heart-centered leadership.

If you are not caring for your people's well-being and mental health, you will not keep them very long. You have to go deeper with people. And here's the secret: it doesn't take a lot to show people you care, but it does take authenticity. Through authentic heart-centered leadership, you can build a team ready to support you and stick with you, regardless of whether it's in the workforce, the sports arena, the PTA, or in your living room.

My experience with coaching has helped me find myself. I now want to pay it forward and help others thrive. Coaching is the best part of my job. I don't care what level people are or where they are in our organization; I love to talk to people and help them unlock the best version of themselves. When I'm done in corporate America, I want to coach full-time for a long time. The gift of helping someone see their full potential and then experiencing the transformation that ensues is amazing.

THE POINT OF IT ALL

I feel happier today than I ever have before. I have been through pain, loss, and suffering, but I also see all the gifts, lessons, and love that came with it. I no longer fear making a mistake and losing everything. I know now where I belong and how to belong. There is always going to be resistance in this life. We have to meet it with the principles of heart-centered leadership. Our experiences can make us close up or be more open. You have to trust your training and believe each experience is meant to serve as a launchpad for you into something greater. Staying open will always be the kinder and often more effective choice.

Life will give you many chances to learn, love, and lead. Too often, we fret over past mistakes or worry that we'll fail in the future. Live in the moment: don't let a fear of failure or rejection stop you from stepping into yourself and your purpose more and more each day. The journey of self-discovery is long, and sometimes darkness and pain meet us on our path: so don't go it alone. We don't get anywhere unless we ask for help and receive it.

Through reflecting on the principles and practices in this book, you'll notice your backbone strengthen and your heart soften. My hope for you is to find happiness, joy, and fulfillment. Get to know yourself, let yourself be seen, and don't look back. The pen is in your hand to write your story. Write it with joy in mind and optimism in your heart, and the magic will find you.

AUTHENTICITY

Steel Backbone:
We often try to hide our emotions and struggles. When we do this, we lose our authenticity and humanity.

What practices can you start today that will strengthen your confidence in truly sharing who you are and what you stand for?

Soft Heart:
Authenticity is a crucial part of being heart-centered. People can sense inauthenticity, and it will put a wall between you and them. Open the door to your heart: let it out for others to see. The cracks you fear are the magnets that invite others to fill you up with support and love.

ACKNOWLEDGMENTS

My mom, Jan: You gave me everything: love, support, kindness. Thank you for always being in my corner, even when I went inward and had to find myself. Your and Ed's love was the wind beneath my wings, then and now.

To my brothers: Scott, Todd, Eric, and Gordon, I loved growing up with you. I always wanted to be around you. Thank you for being great brothers and I look forward to growing old with you all.

Jack: Thank you for being that person who gave my wayward soul a direction. I loved being a wife and becoming a mom. I will always be grateful for our 20 years.

Marlie, Jessie, and Ava: I am so honored to be your mom. You have taught me so much about myself, life, and love. I know I'm not perfect and often feel I have to apologize for not being "a normal mom." Hopefully this book will help you see that normal is not a path for the big-hearted. Be your biggest selves and go light this world on fire.

Aileen: Quietly and thoroughly, you supported me so wholeheartedly during the time after Ed died. Your gentle leadership and friendship were exactly what I needed. Thank you for investing in me and seeing that a slightly different profile of a leader could be just what the business needed.

HJ: Thank you for the depth of care and guidance you provided throughout my coaching journey. Your focus on transformation, in a deep, heart-centered way was truly a life-changer. I am so thankful for all the years we've journeyed together.

Judy: Thank you for opening me up to myself and new possibilities. Your patience with me was and is heroic! Thank you for walking alongside me in a truly supportive manner as I've learned to understand and be grateful for my family of origin. I have loved journeying with you.

Mike: I thank you for loving me so purely. You light up my life, and I can't wait to spend the rest of my life with you.

Mars: Thank you for investing in me and allowing me to learn and grow in a profound way. I had to reflect on my painful story here, yet it is not what I think of working at this company. It is but one story in my arsenal of amazing stories of great people, learning, and developing in a culture that will thrive through all adversity. In my 13+ years, I grew up and am a better person for my time there and will be forever grateful for my experiences.

SmileDirectClub: I thank you for giving me the space and freedom to make a difference and enabling me to truly make someone smile every day.

ENDNOTES

1. https://www2.deloitte.com/content/dam/Deloitte/us/Documents/about-deloitte/us-about-deloitte-uncovering-talent-a-new-model-of-inclusion.pdf

2. "Jolts News Releases." U.S. Bureau of Labor Statistics. U.S. Bureau of Labor Statistics. Accessed January 14, 2022. https://www.bls.gov/jlt/home.htm.

3. Nancy Newton Verrier, *The Primal Wound: Understanding the Adopted Child* (Baltimore: Gateway, 2012).

4. Pema Chödrön, *The Places that Scare You.*

5. H. C. Andersen, *The Emperor's New Clothes* (Richmond, Victoria, Australia: Little Hare, 2016).

6. John Whittington, *Systemic Coaching and Constellations: The Principles, Practices and Application for Individuals, Teams and Groups* (2020).

7. If you are not familiar with this model, take time to learn about it. There are two great books in this space: *FYI for Learning Agility* by Eichinger, Lombardo, et al., and *Becoming an Agile Leader* by Swisher.

8. Brené Brown, *Daring Greatly: How the Courage to Be Vulnerable Transforms the Way We Live, Love, Parent, and Lead* (London, England: Penguin Books Ltd., 2015).

9. Ibid.

10. Rebecca Hinds, "The 1 Trait 94 Percent of C-Suite Women Share (and How to Get It)." Inc.com. Inc., February 8, 2018. https://www.inc.com/rebecca-hinds/the-1-trait-94-percent-of-c-suite-women-share-and-how-to-get-it.html#:~:text=The%20research%20found%20that%2094,between%20athleticism%20and%20business%20success.

11. Ibid.

12. Joseph Campbell, "Where You Stumble, There Lies Your Treasure..." Joseph Campbell Foundation, July 14, 2019. https://www.jcf.org/works/quote/going-down-into-the-abyss/.

13. Sarah Knapton. "Hearts Can Be Kept Alive for 24 Hours after Death, Scientists Have Shown," The Telegraph. Telegraph Media Group, February 14, 2020. https://www.telegraph.co.uk/news/2020/02/14/hearts-can-kept-alive-24-hours-death-scientists-have-shown/.

14. *Moulin Rouge!* Fox Studios, 2001.

ABOUT THE AUTHOR

Cheryl DeSantis is Chief People & Diversity Officer at SmileDirectClub, the fast-growing telehealth pioneer that disrupted the 120-year-old, $12 billion orthodontics industry. With more than 20 years of experience in strategic people and organizational development, Cheryl enables the growth of the business through its team members, striving to maintain SmileDirectClub's strong company culture through values-based leadership. Cheryl has global oversight of talent acquisition, compensation and benefits, team member relations and engagement, business partnership, and learning and development for SmileDirectClub's business across the globe. She also leads the expansion of SmileDirectClub's international internal organizational structure and framework. Cheryl's ability to provide agile and innovative solutions enabled SDC to grow with a business-focused approach that fueled its fast-paced growth yet brought a team member-centric approach to delivering world-class HR programs. This work helped enable SmileDirectClub to receive numerous awards, including being #11 on *Financial Times'* 2021 list of the Fastest Growing Companies in the U.S.

Cheryl is a global thought leader on defining the future of work at SmileDirectClub—a company whose entire business model is based on the belief that virtual connections can be as effective as those in person. She is leading the organization's navigation through its recent progressive embrace of remote and flexible work for good by harnessing the latest technology to keep the team connected, engaged, and motivated. Cheryl has long advocated for inclusion, diversity, and belonging, believing that an environment based on empathy, compassion, and enabling all to bring their full selves to work will drive hard-dollar results. She writes frequently about courageous leadership, vulnerability, and changing the leadership dynamic to be one based on heart-centered and compassionate principles.

Before joining SmileDirectClub, Cheryl acted as Vice President of People and Organization at Mars Petcare, leading enterprise-wide Human Resources programs and policies serving 4,000 employees across the globe. She also was the VP of P&O at the global headquarters in McLean, VA, working with the C-Suite executives on their talent, engagement, and culture agenda. Through her 13+ years of work at Mars, she led benefits and global HR communications, corporate HR initiatives, and long-term people and organizational strategy for several divisions of the business. She was at the forefront of the employer brand work at Mars and also led the cultural integration with The Wrigley Company when Mars acquired them in 2008.

Throughout her career, Cheryl has held positions across many different industries, in disruptive and established businesses, including manufacturing, telecommunications, professional services, e-commerce, and consulting. Before working in the HR field, Cheryl worked in advertising and communications, working on such notable campaigns as Michael Jordan and Warner Brothers on their *Space Jam* campaign. Cheryl lives in Nashville, Tennessee, with her three daughters and two dogs. She was a Division 1 athlete at the University of Virginia, starting all four years and having a leadership role as team captain. For more information, please follow Cheryl on LinkedIn.